Series created by
J. Michael Straczynski

Season by Season

THE COMING OF SHADOWS

Jane Killick

B⬡XTREE

First published in the UK in 1997 by Boxtree Limited,
an imprint of Macmillan Publishers Ltd, 25 Eccleston
Place, London SW1W 9NF and Basingstoke

Associated companies throughout the world

ISBN: 0 7522 2313 5

10 9 8 7 6 5 4 3 2 1

Cover design by Shoot That Tiger!, London
Inside text by Blackjacks, London
Typeset by SX Composing DTP, Rayleigh, Essex

Printed and bound in Great Britain by
Mackays of Chatham, Kent

A CIP catalogue entry for this book is available from the
British Library

Contents

Acknowledgments

This book would not have been possible without all of the wonderful people who gave generously of their time and their comments to make it as comprehensive as it is. I would like to thank them and all the behind-the-scenes people at *Babylon 5* who were so helpful when I was doing my research, especially Joanne Higgins.

Thanks also to Mum and Dad for doing what mums and dads do, and a special thank you to David Bassom.

By Any Means Necessary: Making Babylon 5 on a Budget

*B*abylon 5 has changed the face of television science fiction with its epic storyline, detailed futuristic world, intriguing human and alien characters and its use of computer-generated special effects. But it probably would never have even been made without its ability to stick to a budget. The production model that makes *Babylon 5* possible was so ambitious in the beginning that many people didn't believe it could be done.

Science fiction has a reputation for runaway budgets and it's easy to see why. When a series is set in the future, everything has to be designed from scratch. While a contemporary show might put a desk in an office and dress it with standard objects like a telephone, a desk diary and a computer, a futuristic show has to re-invent everything. If the show has aliens, then they have to have make-up and specially designed costumes. Special effects always add a large slice to the budget, especially with shows set in space, and creating inserts of spaceships or planets costs money. Wandering space shows in the S*tar Trek* mould incur even more expense because they are constantly moving from place to place, requiring a new alien world every week.

Babylon 5's producers knew the reputation of their genre and they were determined not to go down the runaway route that leads to cancellation. At the heart of that determination was the producer John Copeland's production plan. It was an ambitious document right from the start and he remembers that even his own staff – production manager Kevin G. Cremin and production accountant Sarah Fischer – were doubtful when he showed it to them in the first season. 'Both Kevin and Sarah looked at this budget and said, "You're out of your mind. You'll never do this!"'

One or two things gave the production an advantage over other shows, however. The first was getting a commitment for a whole first season of twenty-two episodes. This is extremely unusual for American television, which usually commits for half a season to see how things go, how many people tune in and what the reaction of the advertisers is, before committing to the second half if things go well. The president of Warner Brothers Domestic Television Distribution, Dick Robertson, remembers how important that initial decision was. 'That allowed us to put a lot more money on the screen,' he says. 'We didn't have to pay holding fees to actors; we didn't have to pay holding fees to the guy that owned the building where we produced the show. We could commit up front for twenty-two episodes and the savings on that was probably at least $300,000 an episode.'

It gave the production the assurance of knowing exactly how much money they had to spread over the first season and the freedom to make some big decisions up front. One of the biggest was creating their own studio complex in a warehouse on the outskirts of Los Angeles. At this time, many American TV shows were relocating to Canada or even further afield in search of lower production costs. This would have been more trouble than it was worth for *Babylon 5*. Its reliance on post-production and special effects meant there was a real advantage to staying in LA, where all those facilities are on the doorstep.

'It was more efficient for us to come in here and build three sound stages from the ground up,' says John

Copeland. 'We had way more space and way more control here than we ever would have had [in a ready-made studio facility]. Where we shot the pilot we had two little sound stages side by side. We would just have had those two little sound stages for a whole season. Our main stage with the Observation Dome, the Customs Bay and the Central Corridor is bigger out here than those two sound stages were combined.'

Another thing that sets *Babylon 5* apart from many other shows is the level of planning. While other shows have traditionally learned to cope with last-minute scripts and late rewrites, *Babylon 5* works four or five scripts ahead of time. 'That's one of the very unique facets of this production,' says John. 'Very few other series have the ability to see four or five episodes beyond the point that they are in any given time. You can plan to spend your money that way. We have a budget for the season and we break that down into a pattern budget for what a typical episode should cost – that's our yardstick for production. And we budget every episode. So some of them will be right at that pattern; some of them will be a little less. If we have come under budget on a few episodes, and we know that down the road on episode eight, nine or ten it's going to be really ambitious, we can plan to spend extra money on that. Joe [J. Michael Straczynski, executive producer and creator of *Babylon 5*] always gives me a couple of pages at the beginning of a season which is an outline so I can see where we're going and I can plan for things. One of the fundamentals that we adopted going into this was, "OK, we're going to have to make choices because of the economics we've got on *Babylon 5* and once we've made the choice that means we've decided we're going to do this, and the four things over here we're not going to do."'

'We had to play what we call in American football, "no-mistakes ball",' says Kevin G. Cremin who remained production manager for the first two years. 'We have to not make mistakes. We can't afford to build something and then decide, "We're really not going to shoot it that way, we're going to have our back to that." Everything that we'd built, once we'd committed to it we really had to stay with the idea. There wasn't the luxury of being able to say "Well nice idea, we'll try it later." We couldn't come up with something less than what the producers and directors expected. We couldn't come up with a cheesy-looking prop or a cheesy-looking costume or a cheesy-looking set. We always had to make sure that if we could build a three-walled set and shoot in it and those three walls were going to look substantially better than spending for the fourth wall and then having to downgrade all of the dressing, then that was a decision we had to make.'

In terms of set design, the philosophy of making choices became what the production designer, John Iacovelli, describes as a mantra for the show. He had previously worked with the producers on *Captain Power and the Soldiers of the Future* and was invited to draw up a plan for *Babylon 5* before it was even commissioned because of his reputation for working to a budget. 'The basic elements of doing a show on a budget is knowing what your budget is and being respectful of it,' he says. 'To make choices that are very clear and to make the better choice rather than the idealized choice, to make the choice you know you can win at, not the choice that you know you may possibly lose at.'

Those choices shaped the show in a variety of ways, particularly in John's department, which designs and builds all the sets. 'The money and how little we have of it made so many decisions for us,' he says. 'For example, the idea of putting contrasting colours and values on the sets in a very textural way came from the fact that we couldn't afford the very polished-looking sets that they have over at *Trek* and the other kinds of shows. We just couldn't afford that kind of finish. So my point of view was, like in the theatre, if you've got to hide a bunch of staple holes, wood grain or something like that, then just paint it. It's almost like camouflage. So that was one of the things that drove the show a lot in first season and second season and it became successful – it gave the show a kind of grittier look.'

It is difficult to imagine *Babylon 5* without that grittiness because it fits in so well with the show's fictional reality. At the same time it is a very dark show, which on one level enhances the dramatic mood, while on another serves to protect the viewer from seeing any rough edges.

Another aspect of the show that has helped keep the costs down as far as sets are concerned is the fact that the story is centred on the space station. There are occasional jaunts to Minbar or Centauri Prime, but on the whole the action stays in one place and that means keeping a certain look throughout. A space station of this scale would probably be built using modular components, which allowed John Iacovelli to build these modules and reuse them in various parts of the station. 'I thought that if we had enough of these kind of Lego building blocks, that we could have a lot of different sets. A lot of the scenery, if you're very clever and you're a die-hard fan, you'll see how we put it together. It's a miracle what a paint job can do on a set. In fact when we're designing a set we often think "What do we have?" before "What can we make?" Part of that came from my training in the theatre and being able to do a set for Shakespeare or for an opera, where you have certain elements that are always the same, specific elements that are specific to certain characters, specific to certain groups, and the smallest change can make a huge visual difference. I think the best example of that on *Babylon 5* is the corridors. If we [use the same set, but] change the colour of the stripe and change the number of the corridor, it [looks like] a completely different place. Visually it looks completely different and I get the biggest rush out of that because it's so simple.'

A theatre background is what unites some of the key people on the *Babylon 5* staff. That applies not only to John Iacovelli, but to John Copeland, Ann Bruice Aling and her team of costumers. 'We had all come from a theatre background, so we understand construction, we understand fabrication, we understand budgets, and because we've come from theatre where the budgets are even tighter, we understand being resourceful,' says Ann. 'I think that's helped us in a way that maybe other designers and teams – having come up through television – may not have had that kind of perspective. For me, it always feels like we're doing a big eclectic play every week. It is like doing big theatre that goes a lot faster.

'We have a budget that's doable,' she continues. 'What we did in the beginning was decide where we're going to put our money. So we design and build all of our alien things and some of the principal civilian things, like the Lyta telepath things. We built those and we used to build all of Talia's things, and all the uniforms, anything that's specialized, the Medlab and all that stuff. But for our civilian look, we do buy off-the-rack and we do what I call our "*Babylon* tweak". On men's jackets we take the lapels off and we have strange collar things going on. I buy certain kinds of shirts with interesting geometric patterns on them and we take all the collars off and change buttons. Our background civilians tend to be either very ethnically melting-pot things and a lot of Indonesian and African and South American and Asian garments. Then we mix and match them in strange ways that sort of suggest in the future it will perhaps be more of a melting pot and that keeps it colourful. Then with contemporary humans we start with a basic black underdressing and I just try and find things that are clean, smooth lines, a little bit hip, and we do our little tweak to them. What Joe and John have always said is that our department has really succeeded in putting the money where you can see it.'

Ann admits the first year was 'pretty hellish' when the aliens, the humans and the background characters all needed costumes. Fortunately, many of the principal characters were in uniform most of the time and didn't need a vast amount of wardrobe. That changed over time. 'The principals now all have their closets so to speak, so Sheridan has his bathrobe and he has civilian wear and he has go-to-dinner kind of clothes. But yeah, in terms of our principals, we don't have to augment them too often. Delenn usually gets a couple of things every season and Lennier gets a couple of new things ... For the background, most of the alien stuff has now been built, with groups of Drazi pilots and Drazi merchants and Minbari pilots and Minbari civilians, so it's not just the principals, but the whole worlds that belong to them we have now in stock which we've designed and built.'

Building up a stock of items to use became an invaluable asset for almost every department. Obviously in terms of costumes it means being able to cater for a crowd scene simply by pulling items out of the storeroom. In terms of prosthetics, masks for background aliens become stock items, while pre-existing moulds are available if others need to be made. Even for special effects, once a Vorlon ship or a Starfury has been used for the first time, the model is available in the computer for whenever it is needed again. Stock sets also have a major part to play and, like any other show, *Babylon 5* has its basic sets such as the Observation Dome and the Zocolo which, once paid for and erected on the sound stage, are always there to be used and can even be redressed to look like somewhere else.

But money cannot be made to rule the show. *Babylon 5* is about telling a story and the production has to move to accommodate that. So, in terms of sets, when the war heated up in season three, the Casino set was scrapped and replaced with the War Room. Stock sets can be useful, but are not always appropriate, as in the second season when Sinclair was replaced by Sheridan. 'We had some really nice stuff for Sinclair's quarters in season one,' remembers John Iacovelli. 'I felt really strongly that not only should he [Sheridan] not be in the same physical place but that his stuff should be almost completely different. That was a big expense because I felt visually there were certain things, certain paintings, that we could not use again.'

There are also certain areas where John Iacovelli and his staff try not to scrimp and save. Sometimes it is necessary to spend the money, particularly when it comes to what are known as the 'hero props', things like PPG rifles and links that are going to have significant screen time. 'This stuff is usually in close-up, it's usually next to somebody's face or hand,' says John. 'Definitely with the props and gadgets we try not to scrimp and I think that we do pretty successfully in coming up with interesting-looking things. There's also what we call "the danger zone", which is about three and a half feet up on a set and for the next three and a half feet. That's about where the close-ups happen on the set and that's the danger zone. I talk often to my staff, saying signing should be very crisp there, all the dressing, any wood-screw holes or anything has to be cleaned up. We try to pitch it right around where the actors' faces are because it is television and it is ultimately a show about talking heads. Also, in the graphics I think we've never scrimped. We've always tried to put a lot of money into our graphics because all of us know what a storytelling device that is.'

It was John Copeland's philosophy from the beginning that the story should be king. As far as he is concerned, it is his job to worry about the money and the writers' job to worry about the creative side of the process. 'One of the lessons that I learned as a result of working on *Captain Power*, which had a lot of special effects, [was that] we came up with a lot of parameters of what you could have in a script and what you couldn't have in a script and ultimately this was a handicap for the writers. I wanted us to have a production process that didn't have restrictions for the writers and we just said, "Write the story that you want to tell and we'll figure out how to do it."'

Nevertheless, the show's executive producer, Joe Straczynski, who started out writing most of the episodes in each season and progressed to writing them all, never forgets that he is working within a budget. 'My feeling is if someone hands you $27 million to make a television show it behoves you to act responsibly,' he says. 'So I do try and do things I know we can do, but what generally tends to happen is the production folks come back to me and say, "No, we can do more than this."'

That is exactly what happened with the pilot script, as John Iacovelli recalls: 'I got the first script and there was a very limited number of sets — I wish I could find it because I would love to compare it to the script we ended up with ... Basically I felt that the writing at that moment was being too cautious. I just encouraged him [Joe Straczynski] — I said, "Please don't write knowing that we don't have any money and we don't have any sets: just write what you want and somehow we'll figure it out." I think there's a tremendous trust that's developed between Joe and myself and John Copeland. We know that there's things we won't be able to do, and rarely do we say "Absolutely not, we can't do that" — we find a way to do it. Sometimes we fail. Sometimes I'm just amazed by how good some of the sets look.'

'We're constantly finding the edge of the envelope,' says John Copeland. 'When we find the edge of the envelope, we try to redefine what is an envelope so that we can just go a little further.'

The key moment in redefining the envelope was the development of virtual sets which, over the years, *Babylon 5* has increasingly come to rely on. It has become a hallmark of the series, creating worlds and places that would be too expensive or difficult to do otherwise. The process relates to the way matt paintings have been traditionally used in film and television. Take the case of a scene in the Zen Garden. It would typically begin as a wide establishing shot showing the actors with the computer-generated splendour of the rest of the garden stretching beneath the core of the station. Then it cuts to closer shots of a small part of the garden which is a real set in which the actors perform the scene. That method has been expanded on *Babylon 5* by using Computer Generated Imagery (CGI), which allows whole scenes to take place in sets that don't exist.

'I got a script in the first season and it was for this scene [in 'By Any Means Necessary'] where G'Kar was having a religious ceremony to celebrate an event where the light from the star of his homeworld would reach him at a certain time,' remembers John Iacovelli. 'It was sup- posed to happen in his quarters because that's the only place that G'Kar really had. I read it and I thought, "This is reading like an epic vision, this is reading like some- thing that is bigger." I just couldn't get over it and I went to the director and I went to Joe and I said, "I know I'm going to shoot myself in the foot and I know I don't have any money for another set, but it cannot happen in his quarters. There's got to be other Narns, there's got to be a big huge window to the stars." We had been very cautious of doing windows to the stars because of the whole idea of pressure in space and how expensive it would be to have a window and it's kind of ridiculous to have a window when you can just have video cameras looking outside. But I said, "This needs operatic drama here", so they said "What do you have?" So I said, "What if I provide you with a wall that's only three feet high and a piece of carpet and you guys CGI in the rest of the set – can't you do that?" They looked at each other and kind of laughed and they said, "Well of course!"'

That set became the Sanctuary and has been used on many occasions since, paving the way for other virtual sets like those on Minbar. In many ways it is computer technology like this that makes *Babylon 5* possible. Traditionally, special effects sequences were achieved by building models of spaceships and planets and filming them. Sometimes that might involve filming the models with model backgrounds, for example, if a spaceship had to land on a planet's surface – or it might involve filming models against a blue screen to allow a space background to be matted in afterwards. It would often take three weeks for a special-effects technician to design, build and paint a model spaceship, which is a heck of a long time if it is going to appear in only a couple of shots before being blown up in a space battle. By comparison, creating special effects inside a computer is far quicker and cheaper. It is also more versatile, and has taken *Babylon 5* into uncharted waters in terms of visual ingenuity. Many of the old restrictions that used to dog special-effects designers in television are swept away with the computer's ability to handle things like giant space battles. They would be difficult, if not impossible, to achieve using the old methods.

Babylon 5 has also broken new ground when it comes to filming the scenes with the actors on the set. Typically, an American television drama show will film for eight days of maybe fourteen or sixteen hours a day. A *Babylon 5* episode is filmed in seven days, and those days last no longer than twelve hours. It is something the production team is very strict on, as Janet Greek discovered when she came in to direct her first episode, 'And the Sky Full of Stars'. 'My first day, I went half an hour over and they pulled the plug on me. They all yelled at me and I'm going "What?' I didn't even believe it! But that was the last time I ever went over. I understood what the deal was, that they have to make it for a price.'

It is this aspect of the production that amazes many people in the industry. Comparing *Babylon 5* with an average drama with a typical eight-day running of up to fourteen hours a day, leaves *B5* with an incredible twenty-eight-hour shortfall. 'We had to be that much faster,' says Kevin Cremin, remembering his two years as production manager. 'Our guys had to run that much harder. We had to stay ahead of the shooting company. Much of the time you spend on the set is spent lighting, so if the guys do a degree of prelighting before you get to the set, then you're that much further ahead and you've got a good chance of being able to get your day's material done in twelve hours.'

Then it is a case of using those twelve hours wisely. A lot of that is down to planning and the director will have a week's preparation time to work out the production schedule with the rest of the team. Action sequences always take a long time so these are generally left to the end of the day to ensure all the storytelling material – the dialogue – is filmed first. It sometimes leads to action scenes being curtailed, but that is better than getting to the end of seven days and discovering part of the story is missing. There is also a ban on the expensive and often time-consuming process of location filming, with all its headaches, which can range from getting permission to film, through getting the crew to the location, to waiting for the rain to stop. The other trick is spending time on the scenes that matter, while moving more swiftly with the more pedestrian material. As the director of photography, John C. Flinn III, puts it, 'knowing when to get in and get out'.

He adds, 'And I say that working with the director. I mean, we have scenes that are pretty matter-of-fact: here it is or what's going on. Then we've got the meat. When the meat comes in everybody knows this is where we're going to spend some time and make this thing really aces full.'

John Flinn, who sees how the whole operation works from behind the camera, ascribes the success of making the schedule work to a team atmosphere. 'We know how much time we've got. We're not going to let anybody down,' he says. 'See what a positive thing that is? It's hard to find on any set. When you have workers who are behind it as much as you are, that's exciting.'

Stories of the crew sitting around after work to watch dailies (or rushes) over a pizza or talking about the show over a few beers are common. It is that enthusiasm that aids *Babylon 5*'s success. People want to work that extra bit harder because they care about what they are doing. John Copeland understands that mentality and uses it to his advantage. 'Joe comes up with the vision and I stay in here with the folks and say, "This is where we are going – you get us there,"' he says. 'My job in many respects is to nudge them in the direction that Joe's pointing to and we try to give people the space to find their way to that direction. We don't try to tell Ann [Bruice Aling], 'Look, we want it in corduroy and it's got to be blue with black trim", because if we're defining it that much we're doing the wrong job. Her job is to come up with the wardrobe design and you want to give people the space to do their absolute best work. Everyone has a vested interest in the show; their contribution is paramount and I've always believed that this type of an enterprise is a communal enterprise, that the sum is greater than the individual units. Every cog in the machine is as important as the next cog, from the top all the way down to the runners.'

An important part of the *Babylon 5* machine is, of course, the actors. The show is about telling a story on a grand scale and the size of the cast has expanded to reflect that. It is one of the things that put a strain on the budget. 'And you definitely feel that as a series goes on,' says John Copeland. 'You'll start out with having so many people that are regular that are in every episode and a few more that are in thirteen out of twenty-two, and a few who are in, like, six out of the whole lot. If your series goes on, if you're keeping hold of these actors, everybody has got a contract that is for all shows produced so that they get paid whether they're in an episode or not. That begins to make the budget groan a little bit because your "above the line" keeps getting larger and you have to get a little smarter in how you put the pieces of the puzzle together.'

Fortunately, as cast costs get larger over time, other costs tend to even out a little bit. There is the undoubted advantage of having built up a lot of costumes and sets which can be pulled out of storage as the need arises. There is also the notion of 'practice makes perfect' as people learn where some of the pitfalls are and how they can work more efficiently. That is something the co-producer, George Johnsen, has discovered over in his department, post-production. '*Babylon 5* is an interesting challenge because you're talking about a show where every dollar has to be on screen and mean something,' he says. 'We don't have any dollars to waste. It's one of the few shows where every dollar ends up on the screen, which is a lovely thing to experience, but it does mean that we have to be more thrifty and more facile on how we do stuff, especially in "post".

'Our sound design, our composition and our visual

stuff is all done the most efficient way we know how,' he continues. 'We have explored a whole bunch of new technology to get stuff done, with Christopher [Franke, the composer] having his orchestra in Berlin and mixing it in Hollywood and us having matt painters spread all over the country and animators that are hither and yon. We have figured out a way of bringing all the stuff together to make the show so that it all works.'

In the fourth year, the post-production process changed considerably with the special effects coming in-house. Having it all under one roof has helped George Johnsen extend control over the post-production process for himself and the other producers. 'Joe can come in, and if he's in this area to look at an edit, he can also look at four or five different things that are in progress,' he says. 'He can listen to a sound effect, he can look at a composite that's halfway done, he can look at an idea for animation and put his stamp on it, say, "This is not what I want it to do" before the stuff is all finished. So the rejection process goes down, the collaboration process goes up.'

That has also been true for John Iacovelli and his production design department. 'The first season we would go to Joe a lot and say, "We can't afford this scene." We were very worried about the money, going over budget, and so they would acquiesce and it was very painful to me. I would hate to say to Joe, "We just cannot afford this set; I am sorry, you have to put this scene back in Sinclair's office or Sinclair's quarters because Sinclair's quarters is now the Council Chambers and we don't have time to turn it around." That was painful to me. Now we almost never do that. There's a few things we ask for trades on. We'll make suggestions like "Could this be here because we already have this set up from a previous episode?" – and, to Joe's benefit as a good producer, he's very open to those suggestions. He does protect the show and sometimes says, "No, I'm sorry, it can't be" [if it's important to the story], but more often than not he has looked at it and said, "Yeah, why not?"'

The fourth year also brought some improvements for John Iacovelli's department on a practical level. After three years of working out of little more than an expanded hallway at the end of the sound stages, they moved to the building next door and set up an enclosed construction workshop. 'I cannot imagine how we did it before,' says John. 'We were very tight for storage space: things were stored all over. [There] was the threat of that becoming a fire hazard. And to Skip Beaudine's credit – our production manager – he said, "This must happen; we must have a space to work in." We were losing a lot of productivity during the day because when they're shooting they have a bell when they roll and when that goes off no one can make a sound – you can't even walk. So our productivity's gone up, we've been able to get more done, we've been able to get it painted ahead of time, set it up ahead of time, so it's really been terrific.'

Once the processes were in place, it was easier to come in on budget, and once the series got under way there was proof that it could be done. However, it is still a constant juggling act between spending money and being thrifty, and the final line of defence rests at the desk of the executive producer, Douglas Netter. 'It's always a battle to keep any show within a budget,' says Doug. 'However, we have a wonderful attitude here. We watch the budget very carefully and the attitude from the top is that you can do quality and you can do it at a reasonable budget. We all have the attitude here that we don't waste money, and it comes from me, it comes from Joe, it comes from John Copeland. I know what the costs are in each principal division. When I see any area that is over, I will ask John or Skip why, and there's usually a good reason. If you control costs on a day-by-day basis then you don't get that snowball effect of a series getting away from you.'

It is a measure of *Babylon 5*'s achievement that it has not only come in on budget, but *under* budget. 'It is an element of pride for me to come under budget,' says John Copeland. 'The secret is to not come under a lot. If you come under a whole lot, you look back and say, "Jesus, we could have spent a whole lot more money on these episodes," so you try to ride this razor's edge of spending as much as you feel you can and still pull back a little bit in case you get into trouble.'

Babylon 5 simply wouldn't be *Babylon 5* without the choices that have been forced upon it by budget restrictions. The special effects were produced on a computer in the first place only because it was an affordable way of doing it, and they have given the show more creative freedom than traditional methods. Who could imagine *Babylon 5* without the CGI effects that have become a trademark of the show? Who could imagine *Babylon 5* without the unpolished sets that give it that gritty reality and the low lighting designed to hide the joins? And who would believe that the drama is produced with far less filming time than other shows?

There are moments when the cracks show – of course there are – but that is the same for any show. Even the likes of the *Star Trek* shows with twice the budget and *Space: Above and Beyond* with four times the budget have only a limited amount of money to work with. What the restrictions have done for *Babylon 5* is force the show to be more creative. The attitude is not 'money first' but 'creativity first' and if a problem arises, then a solution needs to be found by thinking around it rather than throwing money at it.

There is no doubt that *Babylon 5* could do more with more money, but at the end of the day, staying within budget means staying on the air. After all, there are many things that attract the audience to *Babylon 5* and money is not one of them.

'Would it be nice to have the extra money? Yeah, I would love it,' says Straczynski. 'I would love to be able to go on location and that kind of stuff, more than we do now. But the story is the characters. Whether this plays out in a garden somewhere or in a room, it's still the characters and it's still the story. So it would be nice, but do I feel tied down or restricted by it? No, I don't.'

BABYLON 5's SECOND SEASON

Babylon 5's second season charts the progress into darkness that is set to engulf the station and the whole of the galaxy. Each new episode takes events nearer to 'The Fall of Night', beginning by hinting at 'The Geometry of Shadows', moving through 'The Long Dark' and racing through 'Dark Places', signs that there is a 'Coming of Shadows' and that Babylon 5 stands 'In the Shadow of Z'ha'dum until it becomes 'Twilight' and the day is ended.

If the first season was about telling stories while setting up the background to an epic saga, then the second season is about playing out events across that background. While in the first season the episodes told individual stories, in the second season they are more like chapters in a book, moving the story forward with each new instalment. Within that, there are still individual stories to be told and, on the whole, *Babylon 5*'s second season had better stories to tell than the first.

Things got off to a bumpy start with 'Points of Departure' and the need to introduce Sheridan and tie off loose ends left behind by his predecessor. 'Points' is easily the weakest episode of the season, but fortunately the second episode, 'Revelations', put things back on track. There is a great variety in the episodes in the first half of the season which concentrates more on telling individual stories than on contributing to the arc. Episodes range from comedy to strong drama, and from those that explore character to those that explore ideas. 'The Geometry of Shadows' has an intriguing idea at its core, introducing the techno-mages with their ability to wield science disguised as magic. There is the horrific idea of a man forced constantly to relive the moment of his death in 'Spider in the Web'. 'Soul Mates' is a great turn for Londo, bringing out the comedy that was part of his character from the start as he deals with the arrival of his three wives. An early dramatic highlight is 'A Race Through Dark Places' which focuses on the Psi Corps and the moving stories of telepaths caught up in its quest for power. Then there is 'The Coming of Shadows', the first major arc episode of the season, in which the Shadows move under cover of the Centauri to provoke war and a change in the fortunes of Londo and G'Kar.

But it is in the second half of the season that the pace really picks up, not only in progressing the arc, but also in the strength of the individual episodes. Exactly halfway through we get 'All Alone in the Night' and suddenly the perspective changes. It sets the tone for the second half of the season, revealing that Sheridan is not all he seemed and putting the command staff of Babylon 5 in a proactive role. After this point, the episodes get stronger and that is true of the stand-alone episodes as well as the arc episodes. Individual stories like 'Hunter, Prey' in which Garibaldi and Franklin go undercover, and the superb 'And Now for a Word', which plays entirely as an ISN news report, demonstrate different types of story-telling and *Babylon 5*'s ability to tell those stories. Then the season ends with a finale of six episodes in which the audience doesn't have time to catch its breath. Morden turns out to have been on the same ship as Sheridan's wife and Delenn tells Sheridan about the Shadows in 'In the Shadow of Z'ha'dum'; the Markab race are wiped out by disease in 'Confessions and Lamentations'; Talia is unmasked as a traitor in 'Divided Loyalties'; the Centauri declare victory over the Narn in 'The Long, Twilight Struggle'; Delenn faces a Vorlon inquisitor in 'Comes the Inquisitor'; and Kosh emerges from his encounter suit in 'The Fall of Night'.

All this time the threat of the Shadows is brooding in the background and it begins with G'Kar's encounter with Shadow vessels in 'Revelations'. He returns to Babylon 5 warning of the return of an ancient and terrible race. This warning goes unheeded by the other ambassadors, but the seed has been planted in the audience's mind and it is one that grows with each further glimpse of the Shadows' power.

In 'A Distant Star' we see nothing more than a Shadow vessel that encounters two Starfuries during their mission to rescue an Earth cruiser stranded in hyperspace. There is no apparent threat here: when the vessel destroys a Starfury, it is more an accident than a deliberate show of force. The Starfury just happened to be nearby when the powerful vessel emerged in hyperspace. This is very much the extent of the threat in the first part of the season. It is something lurking, unexplained, a dangerous mystery to be solved.

In 'The Long Dark', an ambassador from the League of Non-Aligned Worlds talks about the invisible alien creature that arrives on the station as being a 'soldier of darkness'. It is one of many references to darkness that are spread throughout the season. G'Kar tells Na'Toth that he has seen the darkness in 'Revelations', the technomage talks about a coming darkness in 'The Geometry of Shadows', Sinclair mentions it in 'The Coming of Shadows' and Delenn makes several references to it, as in 'All Alone in the Night', when she tells Lennier she will soon be going into darkness. Each reference has a cumulative effect, building on the one before, building the audience's expectations so that when there is finally an explanation in 'In the Shadow of Z'ha'dum', it has a greater dramatic impact.

The Shadows' motives are as yet unclear. All we see is their actions and they are veiled behind the Centauri's attack of the Narn. It begs the question why they want to reawaken the Narn/Centauri conflict. Even Londo is suspicious of their motives and asks Morden what he wants in return for engaging his 'associates' in the war. It is not something that is answered this season. The second season is about the circumstances that lead to war and the consequences arising from it. It is the one strong plot thread that runs through, following on from the attack on Quadrant 37 in 'Chrysalis'. Full-scale war is declared in 'The Coming of Shadows' and officially concluded in 'The Long, Twilight Struggle' with the Narn surrender, although the effects continue to be felt in the episodes that follow.

But while these great events are shaping the galaxy, the focus is really on G'Kar and Londo and how the events affect them. Londo, the washed-out republican of the first season, has been tempted by the promise of power and the prospect of renewed glory for the Centauri. He is well aware of what he is doing – he even asks the 'Great Maker' for forgiveness before starting a war in 'The Coming of Shadows' – but he does it anyway. He achieves his objective and turns the Centauri into a major force to be feared, but he did not foresee the consequences for himself. His victory should be cause for celebration, but it only makes people shy away from him. Even Garibaldi, who was once willing to lend him money to pay off gambling debts, is reluctant to share a drink with him.

It is taken one stage further in 'Knives' when Urza, an old friend of Londo's, calls on him to help his family, who are about to fall victim to Refa's scheming back on Centauri Prime. Now Londo discovers that even Refa, his ally at home, is taking actions that he finds unpalatable. When Urza finds out about Londo's connection with Refa he challenges him to fight to the death, in which Londo kills his old friend, thus saving his family from disgrace. It is a metaphor for what Londo is doing by embracing the power offered to him by Refa and Morden – he is steadily killing off all of his friends.

It comes to a head for Londo in 'The Long, Twilight Struggle', when he is forced to confront the reality of his actions. When he stands on board the Centauri victory ship and looks out on the destruction of Narn, his face turns ashen as he reflects on everything he has done. Earlier in that episode he had told Refa that his 'allies' were beginning to worry him and that things were beginning to spin out of control. But he is still not ready to make a stand. Part of him still longs for Centauri power and when he returns to Babylon 5 after the Narn surrender he shows no trace of regret, only victory.

What makes this so ironic is that the audience feels sorry for him, even after all that he has done. Garibaldi makes this very point in 'The Fall of Night' and Sheridan is surprised that anyone could feel sorry for someone at the centre of an escalating war. Londo was personally responsible for ordering the attacks that killed thousands – if not millions – of Narn and Centauri. At the same time he is caught up in events larger than himself, pulled along by their momentum and isolated by their consequences. The audience cannot help but sympathize with him, and that is what makes his situation dramatically interesting. He should be the out-and-out villain of the piece, but Londo is far more complex than that.

The drama is heightened because Londo must face his enemy, G'Kar, almost every day on the station. While space fleets, generals and resistance fighters continue the war light years away, Londo and G'Kar enact their personal battle on Babylon 5. G'Kar was once the Narn who ranted about destroying the Centauri – now he is the victim of that philosophy. The old G'Kar is the one who plots to kill the Centauri Emperor in 'The Coming of Shadows', but he starts to change when he learns the Emperor is on Babylon 5 to offer the hand of peace. He is suddenly confronted with a possibility he had never considered and, for the chance of a better future for his people, is prepared to put aside personal feuds. When the chance is destroyed by the attack on a Narn outpost, he is ready to kill Londo until he is stopped by Sheridan's cautionary words. This hails the emergence of the new G'Kar, the G'Kar who is able to control his first instinct for revenge and work in more subtle ways which might provide a glimmer of hope for his people. That is reflected again in 'Acts of Sacrifice' where G'Kar faces a group of Narns who plan to kill every Centauri as a message of defiance to their conquerors. G'Kar knows this jeopardises their chances of getting help from the other races and risks his life in a fight to maintain control of the group. He wins that fight, but it doesn't gain him the military aid he was seeking from Sheridan and Delenn, only an escape route for refugees, food and medical supplies.

It would be easy to turn G'Kar into a pitiful figure, but just as Londo is too complex to be written off as the villain, G'Kar has qualities that allow him to maintain his pride even at his lowest ebb. This is someone who fought against the Centauri occupation of his homeworld and now is forced to take a different and more difficult path to resist them a second time. He would rather be back standing with his family and his people when the Centauri attack his homeworld, but he takes the more difficult step of asking for sanctuary on Babylon 5 and that commands both sympathy and respect from the audience. When Narn surrenders to the Centauri and Londo announces his demands to the Babylon 5 Council Chamber, G'Kar is the victim, but when he speaks to the council he maintains a pride and integrity that take the triumph away from Londo's moment of glory.

G'Kar lost his aide Na'Toth in the second season with the departure of the actress Caitlin Brown, who herself had only come in to replace two previous actresses who had had bad experiences of playing female Narns. Na'Toth was played by Mary Kay Adams for a total of two episodes before disappearing. It left G'Kar without a member of his own species to relate to in the way that Lennier does for Delenn and Vir does for Londo. Fortunately, G'Kar's character is so strong that he filled the hole admirably. Perhaps it actually strengthened G'Kar as a character because without someone for him to talk to, the stories had to look for other creative means to express what he was going through. It led to some powerful moments, often without dialogue and particularly when G'Kar was alone, as when he records his final message to put his affairs in order before going out to assassinate the Centauri Emperor, and his urgent prayers in 'The Long, Twilight Struggle', when the Narn fleet is destroyed by Shadow vessels at Gorash 7.

The second season also saw the loss of Talia Winters when, towards the end of the season, the actress Andrea Thompson decided to leave. It brought to an end part of the story that had been developing for two years. Since 'Mind War' back in the first season, there was a suggestion that Talia's telepathic powers were destined to become more significant. The gifts given to her by Jason Ironheart are again referenced in 'A Race Through Dark Places', where, as well as her telekinesis, it seemed he strengthened her overall telepathic power. Sadly, Talia left before those powers could be explored further. There was also her growing relationship with Garibaldi, and particularly with Ivanova, that had to be curtailed more quickly than had been planned. With Talia gone, it left Babylon 5 without a telepath and without the opportunity to develop more stories along the lines of 'Mind War', 'Spider in the Web' and 'A Race Through Dark Places'. Ivanova had neither the will nor the ability to take her place and it would be some time before Lyta Alexander could fill the vacuum on a more permanent basis.

But, to *Babylon 5*'s advantage, Andrea Thompson gave enough notice to turn her departure into an opportunity to tell a good story. 'Divided Loyalties' was strong stuff, merging the themes of conspiracy, telepathy, Ivanova's hidden secret, and the shock of Talia's sleeper personality. It allowed most of the loose ends to be tied up and to suggest possibilities for the future. How much more tragic it would have been if Andrea Thompson had decided to leave the show between seasons without the opportunity to give her character a good send-off.

An addition to the main cast in the second year was Lieutenant Warren Keffer. He was given a place in the opening titles and provided an opportunity to highlight the life of a Starfury pilot, putting himself on the front line for Sheridan and the station. Somehow, his character never really seemed to get going. He was originally going to be introduced in 'A Distant Star', then with a change of plans he was given a brief introduction in 'Points of Departure' instead. Neither of these episodes did very much to establish him as anything more than a minor character. Attempts were made to integrate him into the rest of the crew with forays into the officers' bar, Earhart's, but most of the time his job didn't allow him to interact with the main players in the show. Instead, his individual story arc became the search for the Shadow vessel he had seen in hyperspace. It was more interesting as a plot than it was as development for Keffer, so, when he finally found the Shadow vessel he was looking for in the final episode and got killed, it was no real loss.

The most significant change of the second season, however, was the introduction of Sheridan. It was also the most challenging. The lead carries a show, becoming an integral part unlike any other character. If the audience likes the show then it usually follows that it likes the lead character, or at least has got used to his being there. To then remove him and bring in someone new is going to be unsettling no matter how skilfully that is achieved. Sinclair had grown into an intriguing character over the first season. There had been a pilot plus twenty-two episodes to explore the different facets of his character, from the way he ran the station to his relationship with Garibaldi, his turbulent love life, and, of course, his relationship with the Minbari and the missing twenty-four hours in his life. Sheridan, as far as the audience was concerned, was a blank slate.

It would be fair to say that the transition took time, for the character, the audience and for the actor. His arrival in 'Points of Departure' only really established him as a skilful military strategist, capable of preventing a full-scale confrontation with a Minbari war cruiser. There was nothing yet to make him interesting as a person. A conversation between the command staff at the end of this episode has Franklin commenting that he thinks the new captain is 'OK', and that is very much the audience's response at this moment.

What was needed was for him to become more than 'OK', and that balance is redressed somewhat in 'Revelations'. Here we get some insight into Sheridan the person as opposed to Sheridan the captain. When his sister comes to visit bringing a message sent by his wife shortly before she died, it quite obviously and deliberately invites the audience to sympathize with him and understand him.

The early part of the season then becomes a settling-in period for Sheridan. This is true whether the audience is still clinging to the memory of Sinclair or has decided to go with the flow and embrace the new captain. He deals with problems that arise as one might expect, getting into a couple of shoot-outs in 'The Long Dark' and 'Spider in the Web', making command decisions that do not strictly conform to Earth policy in 'Spider' and 'A

Race Through Dark Places', revealing a little bit more about himself as he remembers the orange blossom in his father's garden in 'The Geometry of Shadows' and wrestling with doubts about his new job in 'A Distant Star'. Then, right in the middle of the season, came 'All Alone in the Night'.

At first it seems like a traditional episode that you might find in any other science fiction show as the captain is captured by some nasty aliens and forced to fight his way out. The reason this sort of story is nothing new is because putting the hero in jeopardy and getting the audience to root for him makes for good drama. Then, at the end, we realize the person we have been rooting for is actually a spy! He is not simply a military man brought in to run the station, but is a man with a hidden mission. All at once there is something more to Sheridan, a hook for his character, and as he takes the rest of the command staff into his confidence, the stakes are raised for Babylon 5.

Bruce Boxleitner, who had the hard task of replacing Michael O'Hare, admits he was feeling his way as Sheridan in those early episodes. And it would be fair to say that his performance grew with the character. He also got some more interesting things to do in the latter half of the season and rose to the challenge, bringing an extra dimension to Sheridan in the interrogation scenes with Morden in 'In the Shadow of Z'ha'dum', in the tender unspoken moments with Delenn in 'Confessions and Lamentations' and in his confrontation with Sebastian in 'Comes the Inquisitor'.

These episodes also continue to raise the stakes for Sheridan. With each step he becomes more interesting, more central to the events on Babylon 5 and the coming 'darkness'. With the revelation that Morden was on board his wife's ship and *survived* in 'In the Shadow of Z'ha'dum' he is shown as a man who will risk everything to get to the truth, and as someone with a personal stake in relations with the Shadows. When the Vorlons send an inquisitor to test Delenn's suitability for the task ahead in 'Comes the Inquisitor', Sebastian is not surprised when Sheridan becomes part of that inquisition. It is just another hint of Sheridan's importance, an importance which is later confirmed when Kosh risks himself by leaving his encounter suit to save Sheridan.

Meanwhile, Sheridan's relationship with Delenn sets up a different thread for his character. As events that are shaping the galaxy revolve around Sheridan, his personal life begins to revolve around this Minbari ambassador. This relationship is built subtly, almost imperceptibly at first, as their lives are drawn closer together by circumstances. It begins in 'A Distant Star' when Delenn meets Sheridan in the Zen Garden and talks about them both going through transitions. It progresses as they have dinner together in 'A Race Through Dark Places' and later 'Confessions and Lamentations'. It is later solidified in 'Confessions', when she takes comfort on his shoulder, and again in 'Comes the Inquisitor', when they declare themselves prepared to die for each other.

Delenn's own story is one of great expectation and great disappointment. She entered the chrysalis backed by the belief that she was fulfilling prophecy, but she comes to realize that her transition has consequences beyond the change in her physical appearance. At the moment she emerges from the cocoon, covered in a crustaceous outer layer, she is frightened about what she has become. That fear evaporates when the shell breaks away to reveal her new self, only to be replaced by the growing realization of what it is like to be neither fully human nor fully Minbari.

It is supposed to be an inspiring transition building a bridge of understanding between the two races, but all she faces is prejudice. The respect she might have expected from her own people is thrown back in her face when Babylon 5's population of Minbari express doubts about her representing them in 'A Distant Star'. During the investigation into Sheridan's shooting of a Minbari in 'There All the Honor Lies', the Minbari witness refuses to answer any of her questions and calls her a freak. Finally, she is dismissed from the Grey Council and mocked by her replacement, Neroon. Of all the people who should have understood her, it was the Grey Council, who knew the prophecy and why she did what she did.

Humanity as a whole also has no wish to build a bridge of understanding with the Minbari, it would seem. It is expressed most clearly in 'And Now for a Word', when the ISN reporter says humans who fought in the war with the Minbari would feel hurt and betrayed to see their enemy with a human face. Delenn breaks down into tears. She has become ostracized from all sides, and apart from Lennier's devotion, her loneliness is complete. It is this that makes her reach out for Sheridan. Only when she has been beaten down as far as she can go in 'Comes the Inquisitor' does she come back ready to fight for her cause, setting both herself and Sheridan on the path to fight the Shadows.

Not every development in the second season was ready to become significant just yet, however. Some of the plot threads from the first season were bubbling under the surface and only popped their heads above water to remind the audience they were there. Among these was the thread containing Babylon 4's mysterious disappearance, brought to the fore dramatically in Season One's 'Babylon Squared'. It is mentioned in 'Knives', adding interest to the story in which Sheridan is possessed by an alien, but doesn't come out again until the third season. Much the same could be said about the conspiracy to kill President Santiago and its implications for Earth. Sheridan recruits the rest of his command staff into a fight to expose the conspirators, but it is a fight that is in no way finished by the end of the season.

Other threads hint at things to come, particularly with the introduction of Night Watch, which serves to make people nervous and causes minor trouble in 'The Fall of Night', but doing little more than lay down preparations for its rise in the third year. The last episode in particular is a lead into what is to come, with footage of the Shadow ship photographed by Keffer being broadcast all over ISN, announcing their arrival to the galaxy, and alerting the Shadows to the discovery of their presence.

Ivanova's voice-over is similar to the one she gives in the opening titles of the third season, indicating a key change in the fortunes of Babylon 5. The second year saw them being battered by the events shaping the galaxy, while the future promises they will fight back, becoming not the last best hope for peace, but the last best hope for victory.

THE
COMING OF
SHADOWS

EPISODE GUIDE

1:
'Points of Departure'

'Commander Sinclair will not be returning to
Babylon 5. He's being reassigned. Permanently.'

Lieutenant Commander Ivanova stands open-
mouthed at General Hague's words. Sinclair is now
an ambassador on Minbar and his controversial
replacement is Captain John Sheridan, known to the
Minbari as 'Starkiller' for destroying their flagship
during the war. He always gives a good-luck speech
within twenty-four hours of taking on a new
assignment, but as he addresses the Observation
Dome staff with those well-rehearsed words, he is
interrupted by an urgent call.

It is from a member of the Minbari Grey Council
who tells him that Kalain, the Minbari commander
of a rogue war cruiser, is believed to be on the
station. Kalain felt betrayed by the Grey Council's
order to surrender at the end of the Earth/Minbari
War and this is the first time he has appeared since
going into self-imposed exile. Sheridan realizes he
must be on B5 for Delenn.

In Delenn's quarters, Lennier kneels before a
cocoon bonded to the wall by a mat of fibrous
threads. Inside, Minbari Ambassador Delenn is
'changing'.

'Get up!' a voice commands from behind. Lennier
turns to see Kalain pointing a PPG at him. He
assumes attack position and stands his ground, until
security arrives and takes Kalain into custody.

Sheridan and Ivanova emerge from interrogating
Kalain to find Lennier waiting for them. He has
been ordered to tell them why the Minbari

surrendered at the Battle of the Line. It was the final battle of the Earth/Minbari War when Earth faced almost certain defeat. The Minbari Grey Council took Sinclair out of the battle, tortured him, interrogated him, scanned him and discovered something terrible. The Minbari believe that when they die their souls are reborn into the next generation, but over the last two thousand years, fewer Minbari have been born and they seem to have lesser souls. 'At the Battle of the Line, we discovered where our souls had been going,' says Lennier. 'Minbari souls are being reborn, in part or in full, in human bodies.'

A Minbari war cruiser comes through the jumpgate on an attack vector. It is Kalain's ship, demanding his release. 'Any attack on this station will be considered an act of war,' Sheridan tells them, but they launch fighters regardless and Babylon 5's Starfuries go out to meet them.

Back in his holding cell, Kalain reaches into his mouth and – with a crack – breaks off a fake tooth. He splits it in half and watches a blue liquid poison ooze out, which he places on his tongue and swallows.

'They're doing everything they can to start a shooting war,' says Sheridan, believing Kalain's suicide is just another step in that plan. Sheridan cannot understand why the station's scanners show the Minbari fighters as clear targets, when that was never possible during the war. And then he realizes what they are doing. He orders the Starfuries to hold position and hold their fire. The pilots protest as they watch the Minbari fighters advance, but Sheridan is firm. 'Continue to hold!'

The fighters fly straight past the Starfuries without firing. Sheridan smiles, knowing the

> *Minbari had wanted the humans to take the first*
> *shot. The warrior caste don't know why the Grey*
> *Council ended the Earth/Minbari War and they*
> *wanted to start it all over again.*
>
> *Later, Sheridan returns to the Observation*
> *Dome. No one is there, but he delivers his good-luck*
> *speech in any case. He finishes and looks out at his*
> *non-existent audience, sighing with satisfaction.*
> *'Five minutes to spare,' he says.*

The introduction of a new captain at the beginning of the second season represented points of departure for both the storyline and the production. The decision to replace Sinclair with Sheridan was, for *Babylon 5*'s creator Joe Michael Straczynski, a necessary thing in story terms. 'My feeling was that Sinclair was the key to the first season of the show, but all his ties were to the Minbari, to the missing twenty-four hours, the Battle of the Line and the founding of the station,' he says. 'I needed someone who had a prior connection to the Shadows but didn't know it and who would also have a way to get into the rest of the story. That character had to be Sheridan, someone new. Lumbering Sinclair's character with that additional material would be stretching credulity to the snapping point.'

Bruce Boxleitner was cast in the role, with a wealth of television experience to his credit. It meant he was very comfortable in a television studio, but he was still the new guy joining an established team. 'I was a little bit nervous about it all,' he admits. 'I heard the usual gossips, who liked who and who didn't and blah blah blah about the other guy. I said, "I don't want to hear any of that." I just looked at it the way that Sheridan would look at it and it actually worked. I'm the new guy here, I've got my orders, I show up, assume my duty as playing this part and luckily we've all gotten along, tremendously so.'

'It was just a breath of fresh air,' says his co-star Claudia Christian, who, as Ivanova, had most scenes with him in the first episode. 'I had never anticipated him being so generous and sweet and talented and gung-ho and all those adjectives. I couldn't say enough about Bruce Boxleitner. He's a true gentleman and an absolute professional and yet he's utterly funny and screws around with the best of us.'

Introducing Sheridan to the audience, giving him a strong entrance that would ease the transition, was something the director Janet Greek was very conscious of. 'And very conscious of helping Bruce through the first episode, establishing his character,' she says. 'He was very nervous and he was very concerned about not making any missteps in terms of what he was bringing to the character. I worked really closely with him on that episode with that. We talked about it a lot and it worked out really well. He's a wonderful commander and does a wonderful job and he can take all the credit for that because he really did his homework – he worked really hard.'

The episode focused on Sheridan's character, which was essential as far as Joe Straczynski, as writer, was concerned. A transitional episode in which Sinclair handed over the reigns to his successor would have detracted from the incoming captain. He decided it was better to make a clean break, contrasting him with Sinclair by making the Minbari openly hostile to him. 'One of the first rules of television is conflict, conflict and more conflict,' says Joe. 'I wanted to up some of the ante here, and not just between Sheridan and the Minbari. We had a crew that got along pretty well together, – Sinclair, Ivanova, Garibaldi and Franklin – and I wondered, "What happens if I throw a grenade into that?" So they aren't sure who they can trust any more. The result of that is you had a lot more interesting conflict between the characters and you learned a lot more about them in the process.'

Of course, with such an abrupt change in command, there was no chance to resolve the story threads that involved Sinclair. The first season had made great play over the missing twenty-four hours in his life and what happened to him at the Battle of the Line. The prospect of this mystery being solved had been teased in 'Chrysalis', the last episode of the first season, and resolved here through a lengthy piece of exposition from Lennier. 'Had he [Sinclair] stayed in the second season, that would have been revealed a little more gradually. It wouldn't have been as rushed. But then it would have hurt the latter part of the season,' Joe explains. 'I would have had to bring in someone else for the Shadow connection and then have him relate to that person. He would have been reduced, more or less, to someone who you would bounce exposition off. So I figured, I'd rather take a short, sharp shot in the first episode than hinder the rest of the season.'

Bill Mumy, the former child star who plays Lennier, remembers filming that scene quite vividly. 'That was Bruce's first day,' he says. 'Bruce knew that I was a real veteran of television, so to speak, so he kind of warmed up to me quick. He knew I'd been around the block quite a lot and also Melissa, his wife, is a very successful ex-child star and we're in a club together. So it was pretty much left up to me – it just kind of ended up that way – to be a liaison with the group of us in making Bruce feel welcome. He got teased a lot the first week or so because there were rumours of his salary bandied about which made everybody else's salary seem like paper-boys'! So if he didn't remember his lines it was, "Oh, and *how much* are you getting paid?" They were really cruel to him – in a good-natured way.'

The scene was aided by the flashback to the Battle of

the Line with Delenn and the rest of the Grey Council standing in their control ship with the fighting going on all around them. As usual, this magnificent sight was achieved with Mira Furlan (Delenn) and the other actors standing in front of a blue screen with the splendour of the battle added in later using computer animation. 'I sat down with Mira and talked to her extensively about what we were going to do,' remembers the director Janet Greek. 'I have to literally paint a picture of every single ship that is going to be in the sky and the battle and where all the fighters were so she knew everything. She's very bright and has a great imagination. All the actors on this show are really challenged that way because there are lots of things that they never get to see and they have to act with invisible partners and everything else. It's not easy. I was never really worried that it would look great because she's really good. I was real happy with the way that came out.'

Once that whole question about the Battle of the Line was resolved, it allowed the matter to be put to rest and to get on with the rest of the story. Joe Straczynski acknowledges this was more or less his intention. 'The information was the information, that wasn't going to change,' he says. 'It was really in the manner of presentation. Do you creep up on it over a couple of episodes, or do you put it out there? It was put out there well enough that I think it works.'

'Chrysalis' had been so packed with cliffhanging story threads that there simply wasn't an opportunity to resolve them all in 'Points of Departure'. So Delenn remained in her cocoon and Garibaldi stayed in a coma. 'You always have fears about your job,' says Jerry Doyle. 'I got the script and I'm in a coma and I'm "Oh, I'm in a coma!" But I got the pick-up for twenty-two episodes for the next season so it was either going to be a long coma or I was going to come out of it and start speaking.

People would say, "What's your favourite episode?" and I would say in character, "Second season; first episode; said nothing; in a coma; full salary!"'

It was a difficult episode to begin the season in that so much had to be accomplished. But with loose ends tidied and a new captain at the helm, the pace was set and *Babylon 5* was ready to move ahead. 'That's one episode where you can most easily see the seams with the first and second season,' concludes Joe Straczynski. 'But those seams vanish very quickly.'

2:
'Revelations'

Five Narn military ships speed through space, being
pursued by a trio of Shadow fighters. The Shadows
fire and two ships explode ahead of them. Two of
the remaining ships turn and advance on the
Shadows, committing suicide so the final ship –
G'Kar's ship – can survive and escape into
hyperspace to tell what he has seen.

Sheridan's sister has arrived on the station and
stirred up memories of his wife Anna. He feels
responsible for her death because, if he hadn't
cancelled their anniversary date, she would never
have joined the crew of the Icarus. 'She never came
back,' he says painfully, 'and I've been noticing
she's gone every minute of every day.'

Lennier enters Delenn's quarters to see her
cocoon cracked open like an egg. He turns to see a
quivering figure covered in a cloak. Could it be
Delenn? She reaches out to him with a scaly, bluish-
grey, shell-covered hand. Dr Franklin comes to help,
but he seems at a loss. He touches her crustaceous
covering and it flakes off in his hand. 'What am I?'
she asks with frightened eyes.

G'Kar addresses the Babylon 5 council with news
of his encounter with the Shadows. He believes they
are the same old and terrible race described by the
Narn prophet G'Quan. 'If true, this holds grave
danger for all of us,' he says.

G'Kar plans to send a Narn ship to investigate the
race's old domain – Z'ha'dum – a plan which Londo
reports to the Shadows' associate, Morden. When
the Narn heavy cruiser emerges out of hyperspace, it

is confronted by a waiting Shadow vessel that blasts
it out of the sky.

Franklin sits by Garibaldi's bedside, rubbing the
tiredness from his eyes. He has tried using an alien
machine to transfer some of his life energy to the
security chief and pull him out of his coma, and
there is nothing more he can do. Then Garibaldi's
eyes begin to flicker and he rises to consciousness.
'Hey,' he manages with a dry, croaky voice. 'What's
up, doc?'

Garibaldi has to know who shot him and uses the
telepath Talia Winters to scan his mind to help him
remember. He flashes back to the moment, and sees
– in that split second before the PPG blast hits his
back – a reflection. As he concentrates on it, he sees
a man's face. The face of his aide.

Garibaldi's aide is easily captured, but when
President Clark hears he is a suspect in the alleged
assassination of his predecessor, he orders the man
to be sent straight to Earth. Afterwards, Ivanova
learns he was transferred onto a ship that isn't
registered with Earthforce. 'So he's gone,' Sheridan
reflects, 'and all the evidence with him.'

Delenn enters the council chambers, the hood of a
white robe covering her face. She walks into the
centre where everyone can see her and she pulls back
the hood. Underneath is a face that is half Minbari
and half human.

Sheridan's sister hands him a datacrystal
containing a message sent by his wife a week before
she died. He places it into the monitor and watches
as her smiling face appears on the screen, talking
excitedly about her new assignment aboard the
Icarus. She says she had already decided to take the
job when Sheridan called to cancel their date, but
she never told him. Sheridan's face is filled with a

mixture of relief, sadness and pain – her death
wasn't his fault. He reaches out his hand to her
image on the screen. 'I love you, Anna,' he says.

'The first episode was really tying up the loose ends and the second episode really puts you back on track for the second part of "Chrysalis",' says Joe Straczynski. 'If you pull the first one out, you can almost jump from "Chrysalis" to "Revelations", but for the introduction of Sheridan.'

The last shot of 'Chrysalis' was Delenn's face barely visible within the cocoon, and this episode reveals the new-look Delenn. The encrusted creature that first emerges from the cocoon seems neither human nor Minbari and meant a long spell in the make-up chair for Mira Furlan. 'Oh my God, that was horrible!' she says. 'I was thinking how lucky I was that I don't have to be like that all the time. That would be a real disaster! The end of a career! The mud girl! You can't breathe; you have glue underneath your nose so it affects you; you always feel like you have a cold. It's very tough to deal with, but it was only for one day and that made it fun, actually. I looked like hell and I still have a Polaroid of me in that make-up reading a beauty section of a magazine, which is really hilarious. It's a great photo.'

There was a lot of debate about Delenn's final look, with Mira more intent on looking completely human, while other designs put forward by the make-up department were more Minbari-like. After a series of discussions with the producers, they went for a compromise. 'I expected Delenn to change almost completely, which didn't happen,' says Mira. 'I still have my prosthetic piece on, which is a strain. I had to have rollers in every morning, and it prolonged my make-up time, believe it or not.'

This change in Delenn had been part of the *Babylon 5*

story arc from the very beginning. Delenn describes the change as a method of promoting understanding between human and Minbari to avoid another war, but its significance goes deeper than that. 'She really had to become genetically compatible with humans,' reveals Straczynski. 'There was a question of why she is doing this and it's because it happened a thousand years ago, unbalancing the souls between the humans and Minbari when Sinclair became Valen. Now she had to reverse that process and go in the other direction and close that door, if you will, which is what she says in "War Without End".'

Delenn's emergence from the chrysalis is just one of several plot threads that the audience is reacquainted with in this second episode. In many ways, it is more of an introductory episode than 'Points of Departure' because it sets us off down the road we are to follow for the rest of the season. The main thrust of the story is G'Kar's encounter with the Shadows and the consequences arising from that. He tells the Council what he has seen and is largely ignored.

Londo, however, secretly reports what he has heard to Morden. 'Here's a guy who's drunk on a little bit of power and who, just like four vodka tonics, can make you do the things you regret in the morning,' says Peter Jurasik, explaining his character's motivations at this point. 'Specifically in terms of that scene, I remember being unhappy. It's one of the scenes I look back on and think "urgh!" I didn't get what I wanted to get out of it. It's the beginning of the second season and I came back to this character and they dressed me all up and put the wig on me and I'm walking around thinking, "Let's see, who is this guy?" So when I look back on that I feel a sense of being unprepared about the scene.'

While momentous things are unfolding for the aliens, more personal things are affecting the lives of the humans. 'Chrysalis' saw Garibaldi shot and slip into a coma and 'Revelations' sees him being pulled out of it using the alien machine introduced in the first season's 'Quality of Mercy'. Like many things that happen in *Babylon 5*, it serves more than one purpose. The fact that it resolves the cliffhanger from the end of the last season is incidental compared with what it sets up for episodes to come.

The dent in Garibaldi's self-confidence when he discovers that it was his own aide that shot him comes to the fore in 'Geometry of Shadows', but there are strong indications of it here when Garibaldi faces him for the first time after coming out of the coma. 'I remember he was sitting by a metal table and I had a cane,' says Jerry Doyle, casting his mind back to the scene in question. 'The first time they said "action" I went to slam the cane down on the table and I hit myself right in the nuts! I went down on my knees and I was like "Oh, oh, *oh*!" So, I finally got the cane figured out and I could use that as a character element, that the character is actually in pain when we shot that scene.'

This was only the second episode to feature Sheridan, and after showing his strategic and military skill in 'Points of Departure', it gives the audience a chance to see a little more inside the man. 'It was awfully quick,' says Bruce Boxleitner, who plays Sheridan. 'I hadn't lived this guy yet and suddenly I was there with the backstory, talking about the wife. Now when I look back on it, it's logical. Joe had to do a lot: he had to catch me up and catch the audience up very quickly to get on with this saga. He had a lot of work to do and I thought he did it very well.'

Jim Johnston, a veteran of the first season, was the director for this episode and also sensed that Bruce was trying to find his feet. 'It was the first time that I worked with Bruce,' says Jim. 'I found him a pleasure to work with because he's a very professional actor and he

comes quite prepared, unlike others. But he was strug-
gling early on to find his niche – which he has, now, I
think. Of course, the commander carries the burden of
the script and he had pages and pages of dialogue. It's
tough not only to learn the lines, but then to bring a performance to them. I think he did a great job.'

'Revelations' takes the opportunity to deepen
Sheridan's character, but as with Garibaldi's coma, it had
a further purpose which Joe Straczynski is keen to
stress. 'A lot of people thought I was trying to give him
some characterization by giving him this wife that had
passed away and that was all we were going to hear
about it. Of course, this was setting up a very important
part of the arc that would play out until the rest of the
season – and then some.'

The episode concludes towards the end with an
excerpt from W. B. Yeats's poem 'The Second Coming',
which acts as a kind of prophecy for the course of the
show. Yeats was not, of course, writing about the
Shadow War, but the images of things falling apart and
anarchy being let loose on the world are very apt to that
situation. What makes it more interesting is that the
words of the human poet are spoken by G'Kar.

Andreas Katsulus, who plays G'Kar, has no special
interest in poetry, but found the meaning in the words. 'I
think in acting we become sensitive in these things,' he
says. 'There's a power in that poem and almost a parallel something with the universe *we're* talking about and
the universe that *it's* talking about. What was going on is
G'Kar is softening up to the humans and not stereotyp-
ing the humans – what would be the equivalent of black
people think all white people are bigots and all white
people have this notion about black people. So we've got
Narns who think all humans are "yadda yadda yadda ...",
then setting that attitude aside and saying, "If a human
can have written this, maybe they're not all so bad."'

3:
'The Geometry of Shadows'

'Great Maker!' gasps Londo as he sees a man in a black cloak enter the customs area. He is a techno-mage, a member of a rarely seen sect who use science to achieve the effect of magic. 'To see more than one of them at a time is considered a very bad omen,' says Londo as two more join the first.

Sheridan promotes Ivanova to commander and gives her a first job of sorting out the problem of the Drazi, who have begun fighting all over the station. They've split into Green and Purple factions by pulling a coloured sash out of a barrel in the traditional manner. Ivanova is astonished and, by way of an example, takes a purple sash off one Drazi and puts it on a green-sash-wearing Drazi. Within seconds, the whole place has erupted into violence. Two wrestling Drazi dive on top of her and she screams as her foot is broken in three places.

Garibaldi sits in his quarters contemplating his PPG. He slots the energy cap into the gun and listens to it power up. Then he removes it and begins the process all over again. He is interrupted by Sheridan, who wants to know when he will be returning to work. 'I don't know,' says Garibaldi. 'Maybe it'd just be easier on everybody if I just resigned and moved on.'

Londo feels that if he can be associated with the techno-mages, it will improve his standing back home. They rebuff his request for a meeting, so he manages to sneak into a meeting that Sheridan has.

But the techno-mage is wise to the recording device that Londo has surreptitiously placed in the room, and, with one glance, destroys it in a flare of sparks.

The techno-mage later tells Sheridan of the great knowledge safeguarded by his kind, a knowledge they plan to protect by journeying far away. 'There is a storm coming,' he tells Sheridan. 'A black and terrible storm. We would not have our knowledge lost or used to ill purpose.' As he leaves he places an orange blossom in Sheridan's hand. Sheridan marvels at the little white flower, just like the ones that used to fill his father's garden with their scent when he was a child.

Garibaldi emerges from his quarters to catch Lou Welch and a team of security guards on their way to Brown sector on orders that were uplinked by Ivanova. Garibaldi is suspicious. 'An uplink? Not a personal message?'

Garibaldi raps on the door of Brown 2 and goes into his salesman routine with the confused Drazi who answers his knock. Ivanova hears his voice from where she is tied up out the back. 'Garibaldi!' she screams and thrusts her elbow into one of the Drazi beside her. Between them, they manage to take out the rest of the Drazi guards.

Garibaldi and Ivanova manage to block the way of the Green Drazi who are en route to kill their Purple opponents. Ivanova yanks off the Green leader's cloth, saying the whole thing is insane. He looks back at her, totally shocked. 'Who takes cloth for Green leader is Green leader,' he says and stands to attention. Ivanova ties the sash around her neck and leads the Green Drazi off to find some purple dye.

Babylon 5's security team hold a party for Garibaldi to celebrate his return to work. Saving

Ivanova made him realize he has two unique qualifications for the job: he has an intimate knowledge of everyone and everything on the station, and he doesn't trust anybody.

The Drazi episode emerged out of Claudia Christian's request for another episode that allowed her to play a bit of comedy. 'I had a great time because the actors were extraordinary and it was just funny,' she says. 'For Ivanova to be so exasperated and frustrated, thinking she had the diplomatic solution to everything and finding out she didn't. That was a fun episode for me.'

The episode also saw Ivanova break her foot, something that only entered the story when real life intervened. 'I was chasing a bird in my garden – it's the truth!' says Claudia. 'I was happy and I was running around like a little kid and I did a flying ballet leap and I landed incorrectly on a stone and my foot crushed in four places. I think a ghost tripped me or something bizarre like that because I can't imagine a little ballet leap would do that, but it did. And then, after the incident, I came back from the hospital and – since I don't take any pills of any sort, not even any aspirin – I proceeded to drink myself out of my pain. I had a whole bottle of red wine and called John Copeland [producer] and said [in a slurred voice], "You're not going to believe this: I broke my leg." They said, "Don't worry about it, we'll work around it." And sure enough he rewrote the episode – and very quickly, I might add.'

The rewrite required that Ivanova actually be seen breaking her foot, which was the worst bit for Claudia. 'Just shooting the actual scene with the stuntman falling right next to my already broken foot to make it look like he was falling on my foot in order to break it – *that* was frightening. When you break something the last thing you want is somebody even near it. You're, like, paranoid: you want ten feet of space around you at all times. So to have somebody "boom!" right next to my crushed foot, I had to really work beyond that to act like I wasn't flinching.'

It was originally planned for Ivanova to fight her own way out of trouble when she was captured by the Drazi. Her broken foot meant Garibaldi was brought in to help her out. Other changes were relatively minor and Claudia even acted some scenes walking unaided on her plaster cast. 'It was exceedingly painful the first few days,' she says. 'They were so sweet, though. They built me some special wide stairs for my crutches and a handrail on my trailer. People were very kind. People would bring me bags of ice all day long and tell me to put my foot up. The crew was unbelievably generous and sweet and careful.'

Ivanova clearly considers the Drazi Green and Purple conflict to be an absolute nonsense, even if they have their own cultural reasons for the feud. Parallels can easily be drawn with human conflicts, whether they be based on the colour of a person's skin, their religion or their territory. The parallel Joe Straczynski draws is with the ethnic civil war in former Yugoslavia. 'Wars are often fought for reasons that are relatively trivial in hindsight,' he says. 'When you look at what was Yugoslavia – OK, you're Croat, you're Serb, but you're in the same country. You've been there for centuries and suddenly one day, because a word changes, you're enemies and the person who was your next-door neighbour suddenly you want to kill. I thought, "How trivial can I make this? How stupid can I make this?" That they would arbitrarily divide up and fight with each other every five years appealed to me to show the stupidity of a lot of war and the divisions that come up.'

It was, however, the techno-mages that really captured the imagination of many viewers, purely through the idea that magic could be created using technology. 'It's a concept that I found fascinating,' says Joe. 'In a way, there was inspiration for this in Arthur [C.] Clarke's comment that any sufficiently advanced technology is indistinguishable from magic. I thought, "What if you pursue this to its logical conclusion and say that this is technology that replicates magic?" Every so often I do ideas which I think are cool, and this is a cool idea.'

Vir comes up against the techno-mages when Londo asks him to request an audience with them. Their first response is to try to scare him away by conjuring up a giant monster. The monster was, of course, created in a computer. It meant that the actor Stephen Furst had to stand there and imagine the monstrosity in front of him, which he finds one of the more challenging things about being in *Babylon 5*. 'I had never done a science fiction show before and what's difficult sometimes is trying to act, not with other actors, but with things that aren't there, like being chased by the techno-mages. They're coming at you and you're supposed to be scared and there's nothing there – just a guy with a little cardboard stick. And that's kind of difficult.'

Londo sends Vir to the techno-mages because he thinks it will increase his status among the Centauri. His ambition is overflowing at this point, bolstered by his involvement in the destruction of the Narn outpost at Quadrant 37 and by Refa's reports of what they are saying back home. This is a Londo who is still unaware of the consequences of his actions. 'It's my very favourite episode that I've done,' says Peter Jurasik, who plays Londo. 'For me, it was successful almost in every scene. I felt really good about all the scenes. I liked the episode because I played on a number of different facets of his character. There was some very funny stuff that he had to do. There were some very serious overtones. There was some real conniving and desire for power, manipulation of fear, which becomes a bigger issue as we go into the series arc, but that starts there, using Vir.'

'The Geometry of Shadows' sees Garibaldi at his lowest point. After being bounced around from station to station, he finally has his drinking problem under control and has settled down into a job he is good at. Then he is shot by his own second in command and wakes up from a coma to find the one person who trusted him enough to give him the job in the first place – Sinclair – has been reassigned. In ordinary episodic television, a character might get shot one week and be as right as rain the next. That's not the case with *Babylon 5*. When Garibaldi comes out of his coma, his body may have recovered, but it takes a lot longer for the mental scars to heal. 'The primary theory of drama is you put your characters up a tree and throw rocks at them as much as you possibly can,' says Joe Straczynski. 'Garibaldi is a character who does not trust easily or well. Having someone who he had trusted, and who we saw throughout the entire season who was sort of there turning on him, knocked him through a bit of a loop to the point where he wasn't sure any more what he wanted to do. I think it's that episode where you have the scene where Garibaldi is considering blowing his brains out, so it really does shake up his whole world.'

The scene in question is where Garibaldi is taking the energy cap in and out of his PPG. 'That was a weird one because the audience thinks that I'm thinking about killing myself. I wasn't,' says the actor Jerry Doyle. 'Then Sheridan came in and Bruce gave me a look. I wasn't planning on going in that direction, but he gave me something and I fired off that. So the scene took on a whole reality that I hadn't planned on in the beginning, and I think it worked.'

This part of Garibaldi's life is just a mini-arc within the greater whole, but it demonstrates how *Babylon 5* uses the episodic format to build tension and build an issue over several episodes. And while other shows might forget that something like this had ever happened to its characters, this experience will always be a part of Garibaldi's background, with the risk that it may rise to the surface again in the future.

4:
'A Distant Star'

Captain Maynard stops off at Babylon 5 with some
wild stories about the things he has seen in
hyperspace while aboard his explorer-class starship,
the Cortez. 'There's something out there,' he says,
'and it's stranger than any one of us can know.'

Sheridan finds his old friend Captain Maynard has
awakened doubts about his life on Babylon 5. Being
a bureaucrat dealing with the everyday squabbles of
alien races is not what he trained for. Sheridan is a
starship captain who has found himself tied to a
desk and doesn't know if he is right for the job.
'Maynard was right,' he concludes. 'I've been
beached.'

Franklin's decided Garibaldi needs to go on a
diet. 'C'mon, doc! No salt, no bread, no anchovies?'
Garibaldi protests. But Franklin insists he stick to a
food plan to aid his recovery, even if that means not
making his favourite meal, a kind of Italian fondue
called bagna cauda.

The Cortez leaves Babylon 5 behind and returns
to hyperspace. All is well on board the ship until a
spike in the fusion reactor sets off an explosion on
the bridge. Sparks and bodies fly everywhere, and
flames rage from one of the lower consoles. The
crew pull themselves to their feet to discover they've
lost their lock-on signal from the jumpgate and they
are stranded in hyperspace.

A garbled distress signal reaches Babylon 5, but
Ivanova is less than optimistic about saving them.
'No ship lost in hyperspace has ever been found
again,' she reminds Sheridan. But he knows he has

to try, and sends out a squadron of fighters to bring it back home.

The Starfuries stretch out in a lifeline through hyperspace until they latch onto a faint, garbled signal from the Cortez. As soon as they make contact, a huge ship – black and spindly like a giant spider – appears out of nowhere, passing so close to the first fighter that its sheer power shatters the tiny craft into pieces. The second fighter spins out of control and loses its lock on Babylon 5, leaving its pilot, Warren Keffer, stranded. All he can do, as his Starfury tumbles in hyperspace, is guide the Cortez back by firing in the direction of home.

Sheridan stands in the Zen Garden, thinking about the lost pilots. He is joined by Delenn. 'They saved others,' she tells him. 'They were in the right place, and knew what to do. As you did.' As she talks, she begins to wipe away Sheridan's self-doubt. The universe, she says, puts people in places where they can learn, and all the molecules in the universe, including those that make up their bodies, come from the stars. 'We are starstuff. We are the universe, made manifest, trying to figure itself out. And as we have both learned, sometimes the universe requires a change of perspective.'

Another giant black Shadow ship appears in hyperspace. It is in Keffer's view for only a moment, but its flight path gives him enough to compare it with that of the other ship and figure out a way home.

'Did you get it?' Garibaldi anxiously asks Orwell, a freelance retailer down at the cargo bay. Orwell pulls the lid off a box in front of him and reveals all the ingredients of bagna cauda. Garibaldi's delight is halted when he is caught red-handed by Dr Franklin. Garibaldi explains that his father used to make *bagna cauda for him on his birthday and now, every year, he makes it for himself to honour his dad. 'Well, in that case,' Franklin smiles, 'why don't you make enough for two?'*

The idea for 'A Distant Star' came from a premise by J. Michael Straczynski, who passed it on to Dorothy C. Fontana to expand into a full story. 'It was half a page of "Here's what happens: a ship is lost in hyperspace and they had to figure out a way to get it back",' says Dorothy. 'It was not very detailed. I came up with the captain – in fact he's named after the father of a dear friend of mine.'

The arrival of Captain Jack Maynard forces Sheridan to reflect on his position. Maynard is an old friend of Sheridan's, a man he admires and a man who is doing the job that Sheridan trained for. In contrast, Sheridan is stuck behind a desk and it makes him wonder if it is the right place for him. 'I agonized over that story a little bit,' says Dorothy. 'A new character, a new captain, you didn't know much about him. I knew Bruce Boxleitner's work, but who is Sheridan? My episode was fairly early in that season and I finally figured out what Sheridan's problem was. Sheridan's problem had to be, "What am I doing here? This isn't my job." Once I figured out what Sheridan's personal problem was the rest was OK, because otherwise in that story he would be saying, "We have to get that ship back. Go get that ship back." This gave him something more personal to agonize over, and in making that adjustment I think he became more interesting.'

Sheridan has many self-doubts over his abilities in 'A Distant Star', but if the events show anything, they show how right he is for the job, and this is what Delenn points out. If it wasn't for Sheridan, the *Cortez* may have remained lost in hyperspace. He came up with the plan to save it and thereby achieved something that nobody else had ever done before.

There are certain parallels between Sheridan and Bruce Boxleitner who, like the character he plays, had to settle into his new surroundings. At first he was the new guy surrounded by a group of actors who had had a whole season to establish their characters. By 'A Distant Star' he had started to settle in and get excited by the story unfolding around him. 'By the fourth episode I had a grin from ear to ear,' says Bruce. 'This, in my time of life and career, it just answered everything wonderfully. This just sparked my imagination because it's not like doing regular network television. You're dealing with a much more imaginative world than normal. I hadn't done a lot of science fiction and you're dealing with much more theatrical themes – it's larger than life. We don't deal with who's sleeping with whom, à la Melrose Place. We're dealing with galactic wars and empires and creatures from other places.'

Another new character for Season Two, Lieutenant Warren Keffer, was also finding his feet in this episode. As Dorothy Fontana remembers, 'A Distant Star' was originally going to be his introduction. 'Then Joe called me and said, "No, we've decided to introduce him earlier so anything you have that is introductory for him, forget it." I said, "OK, fine." So that required a little rewriting and redevising in the second draft.'

Adding Keffer into the mix of *Babylon* 5 allows the storyline to visit the grass-roots personnel on the station. By focusing on him, the audience gets an insight into someone on the front line who is facing the consequences of Sheridan's orders. Sheridan acknowledges he is asking the fighter pilots to put their lives on the line when he sends them out into hyperspace, and it is something Jim Johnston wanted to emphasize when he directed that sequence. During Sheridan's long speech, he kept the shot moving by circling around the pilots to show their faces. 'I try to break those up, use steadicam a lot rather than be on Sheridan, who's delivering instructions,' he says. 'In World War Two footage I see the guy briefing the pilots before they go over and bomb Germany and there's just as much interest in those who are about to die, how are they taking all this, than on the guy who is going on and on. Also, I think it holds people's interest when you're moving the camera and showing them something different.'

During the mission, two of the pilots encounter a Shadow ship so powerful that it destroys a Starfury just by passing close to it. But at this stage it is still an unexplained phenomenon, a mystery to be resolved and to keep viewers wondering what exactly the 'something' is that both Maynard and Keffer saw in hyperspace. The episode also served a useful function by explaining a little bit more about the way hyperspace and jumpgates actually work.

The subplot came from a line in the original premise which said that Garibaldi had to be on a special diet because of his recent injuries. Dorothy Fontana used it to lighten the mood by bringing in Garibaldi's quest for the ingredients of *bagna cauda* – a favourite Fontana family recipe – and putting Ivanova and Sheridan on a diet as well. 'That was ironic,' laughs Claudia Christian. 'I had to say, "Look at me, there's not an ounce of fat on me." I do work out and I eat very healthy, but by all means I'm not a size two! I'm a regular size eight, five-feet-nine girl, and for me to say that, I had to think "OK". It made me seem like I was some sort of Schwarzenegger thing!'

Things take an unexpected turn for Delenn. Having made the change to build a bridge between humans and Minbari, she finds herself being distanced from her own kind. A representative from the other Minbari on the station tells her that he is not sure if she is really one of

them any more. The sentiment holds a personal resonance for the actress Mira Furlan, who has lost a sense of
belonging since leaving the former Yugoslavia in the
midst of the civil war that split the country. 'It's incredibly close to my heart because that's what I feel in terms
of this whole madness in what was once Yugoslavia,' she
says. 'I really feel that I don't belong to any of the groups.
I don't. I mean, I'm such a mixture of everything. But it's
not about that, it's not about genetics: it's about your
own feeling ... I don't belong to America, certainly. I'll
never be an American. What am I? A Yugoslav? That
doesn't exist any more. The world and the Yugoslav
peoples have said that that doesn't exist. Am I a
Croatian? That whole thing of blood and belonging is not
something that I can relate to. I've always felt like a citi-
zen of the world. It's a very hippy attitude, but that's how
I feel and I think that people have a right to feel that way
... It's something that I really feel deep in my own life, so
I guess that reflects on screen.'

Delenn's contemplation about her place in the universe gives her a certain understanding of Sheridan's
predicament when she tells him they are all made out of
the same material, they are 'starstuff'. 'That's what fans
always want to hear and I love it, it's great, it's very
poetic,' says Mira. 'Also, in a bigger way, it speaks about
the same issue of not belonging as we are all part of one
thing, all of us. Whether we speak this language or that
language or have that colour of skin or this colour of skin
or a bone in our head and no eyebrows and so on, we're
still a part of this big huge thing. That's what people
forget and that's why there is trouble.'

'Every so often I try and play [with the notion] that life
is miraculous in some form or another,' says Joe
Straczynski who added the 'starstuff' concept to the
episode. 'Being here is a form of wonder, whether it is
the universe trying to understand itself, or what have

you. It's an attempt to say that your life is not a mundane thing. Yeah, crappy things happen to you, but you're made of the same material as stars. The universe said one day, "I am going to try and figure myself out", and you're here because of it. There's enough out there that trivializes life – let's make life special.'

5:
'The Long Dark'

*Beams of light search through the interior of an
ancient ship that has limped its way towards
Babylon 5. The* Copernicus *came from an Earth
before jumpgate technology when travelling into
deep space meant going into a frozen cryogenic
state. The searchlights reveal two cryogenic
chambers. Inside one is a hideously decomposed
body with a face that seems to have frozen in fear.
In the other is a woman, and she is alive.*

*'Judgement day is coming!' screams a lurker at the
uninterested crowds in the Zocolo. 'I have seen it!
An army of darkness, soldiers of the devil!'
Garibaldi grabs him firmly by the arm and leads him
to the cells, where he can sleep it off. The lurker,
called Amis, is disturbed by bad dreams that take
him back to his past as a Ground Pounder in the
war, reliving the attacks as he talks in his sleep.
Garibaldi looks down on him with sympathy. He
has had the same dream.*

*The woman from the cryogenic tube, Mariah
Cirrus, wakes up in a world a hundred years in
advance of the one she left. Franklin takes her on a
tour of the station to show her all the things she has
never seen before. Including aliens. G'Kar holds out
his hand in greeting and she stares into his red,
lizard-like eyes. She takes his hand for a moment
and then flinches in pain. A vision whips through
her mind. Something monstrous that she can hardly
see is moving in on her as she lies in the cryogenic
tube. She screams and faints.*

Mariah wakes up in Franklin's quarters to find

*the doctor watching over her, stroking her hand
tenderly. He tells her that her husband, who was in
the other cryogenic tube, was murdered by
something on the ship. Mariah is frightened,
confused, out of her time, alone. Franklin tries to
calm her. She is not alone, he says, and they kiss ...*

The League of Non-Aligned Worlds insists the
woman be removed from the station. 'She has
brought something evil from the past,' says the
Markab Ambassador. 'A soldier of darkness.'

Amis can sense it. When he was a Ground
Pounder his whole unit was killed by something that
came out of a storm on a small moon in Sector 797.
Only he survived. 'It kept me alive as a snack,' he
tells Garibaldi. 'That's how I knew it was here. Part
of me is still inside that thing.'

Garibaldi chases after Amis and finds him
suspended in mid-air by some unseen force.
Garibaldi fires at it and Amis drops to the ground.
Sheridan, Ivanova and a security team join them,
having been alerted by the PPG fire. They aim their
weapons and fire in a concentrated burst. Sparks of
energy flash across the alien, revealing the outline of
a body. It writhes as the fire continues, the energy
beams showing an alien body with arms, legs and a
monstrous head. It collapses to its knees and turns
into a cloud of energy that disappears into
nothingness.

With the alien destroyed, Franklin asks Mariah to
stay, but she has decided to go back to Earth. She
kisses him lightly on the cheek and walks out of
Medlab and out of his life.

The Copernicus's records show it flew past the
same moon that Amis was stationed on during the
war and then changed its course. It was
reprogrammed to journey to the exact place where

*G'Kar said an old enemy was gathering its forces –
Z'ha'dum.*

The initial premise for 'The Long Dark' was that a servant of the Shadows arrives on Babylon 5 on its way to Z'ha'dum. In the telling of the story, this aspect became a small part of the whole, as the episode concentrated on the two characters that the alien servant fed on to keep it alive. It keeps the undercurrent of encroaching darkness in the background, while other events – more trivial in the whole scheme of things – hold our characters' attention.

For Franklin, it is the woman who arrives on the ship from the past. She is out of her time, she has lost her husband and she is suffering trauma from what she endured in stasis. Franklin treats her first as a doctor, then as a friend and finally as something more.

'I didn't quite know how that came off,' says Richard Biggs, who plays Franklin: 'if the doctor was attracted to her, or whether Franklin was guilt-ridden about being attracted to her, or if he just wanted it to be a doctor–patient relationship. I didn't quite know if she was attracted to him or if she was just in mourning for her husband. I didn't quite know how that played and I talked to Joe and I told him I was having some problems and Joe said that there was a fine line and he wanted the audience to wonder if Franklin's emotions were getting in the way of him being a doctor to a patient. So that's what I was trying to play.'

Mariah is a fish out of water and, as Franklin introduces her to the station, it has the advantage of re-acquainting the audience with some of the background to *Babylon 5*. His explanation of how the Centauri were the first alien race to contact humanity, how humans reached out into space and how they have fared in the brave new world was useful exposition for the early part of the season. In a different way, this is also what the character of Amis does, revisiting the issues of Downbelow and the Earth/Minbari War.

Amis is a lurker, one of the forgotten members of society who scrape a living in the undeveloped parts of the station. The attitude of many people, voiced by one of Garibaldi's guards, is that they are good-for-nothings who should be dumped into space. But the episode demonstrates that this is a short-sighted view. Amis used to be a soldier who fought in the Earth/Minbari War and was turned crazy by his experiences. The security guard only sees a waster from Downbelow, but the truth is he has served his people in a way the guard has not, and, through no fault of his own, has been left on the scrap heap.

Garibaldi shares a past with Amis as they were both Ground Pounders who came through the war. The only difference is that Garibaldi was able to come out of it with some sort of a career. Garibaldi's part in the war had always been in his background, but this is the first time we find out what his role actually was and he gets the chance to open up a little about his experiences. It is Amis who does that for him because Garibaldi sees a part of himself in him. There is a sense in which Amis is the person he might have been if he hadn't controlled his drinking problem.

Dwight Schultz, best remembered by TV audiences as Mad Murdock in *The A-Team*, played the crazed and frightened character opposite Jerry Doyle's Garibaldi. 'It's funny how this town has preconceived notions,' says Jerry. 'I hadn't been in town that long, I'm not well-schooled in actors' names and TV shows and films and all that kind of stuff and it ended up I was working with this guy who was on *The A-Team*. And I was like "*The A-Team*?" Christ! I'm thinking everybody's Mr T, you know?'

But all his preconceived notions were swept away when filming started. 'I tell you, Dwight Schultz came in here and just rocked me. He was so good. I had so much fun working with him. A very nice guy, a very good actor. I can't say enough about his performance. It was outstanding.'

The third guest character is the alien itself, seen only by the outline of its body created by the energy from a hail of PPG blasts. The director, Mario DiLeo, admits being inspired to portray the creature in this way by the classic 1956 science fiction film *Forbidden Planet*, in which the monster's invisible body is revealed in a similar way. 'They wanted to materialize something, to see a hand or something,' he says. 'I didn't want it, so the producer accepted the idea to make it like a force. It worked well, I think, because it had suspense.'

Once the decision had been made to make the alien invisible, it allowed its presence to be felt even when it could not be seen. For example, when Mariah is brought on board the station, there is the sense of the force following her, watching from above as she is taken to Medlab. It also spies on Ivanova from above as she surveys the *Copernicus* alone. 'I used a remote camera system that is put on a boom,' explains Mario DiLeo. 'With that system you can use high camera angles and long takes using different camera angles. You need this bird's-eye point of view for the energy field, the energy field being taller than the regular person. You can achieve those angles by using other tools, but the other tools take much more time.'

It led to the climax where the station staff are forced to attack something they can't see. But for the cast, it was just a normal day at work interacting with computer-generated images that would be added later in post-production. 'Those scenes are always weird to shoot,' says Jerry Doyle, 'because you're shooting at something that's not there with guns that don't work!'

However, it was this last scene which let the episode

down for Joe Straczynski. 'I think it was fairly well developed by the writer [Scott Frost],' he says. 'Where it falls down for me is in the effect at the end. We had planned something far more substantive and surreal-looking than what we got. It would have been nice if we could have got what we had planned on because you have this great build-up and it doesn't really pan out as well as it might.'

The last two scenes put a different spin on the episode. In Ivanova's revelation that Mariah's ship was heading towards Z'ha'dum, the alien becomes more than a creature that preyed on humans: it becomes a warning. Suddenly, the fears of the League of Non-Aligned Worlds that it is a soldier of darkness have greater resonance. It also gives credibility to G'Kar's warning about the return of an ancient enemy. It is emphasized in the final scene when we see G'Kar in his quarters with the Book of G'Quan, looking at a drawing of a black shadowy enemy.

This is the first glimpse in the second season of G'Kar's wonderful chest and arms. It makes his Narn physiology more convincing, but involves more prosthetic work for the actor. 'If having glue all over your face isn't enough, when they suddenly announce they want to put glue over your chest and over the hair on your arms ...! You can't play the pain you are in,' says Andreas Katsulus. 'And then, timewise, everyone has a certain amount of patience to sit in this passive state [being made up]. It's very agreeable, and I use that time in a positive way to prepare, but enough is enough! I don't need more than an hour and a half preparation, so when it's doubled – and even beyond that! – it's just sitting there and steaming! It's a lot of work for an effect. I guess it's to make the world we're creating seem real in all its detail. It's like, "My God, this world is real down to the nitty gritty". So you have to pay that price of the discomfort in order to do it. I ask Joe to do it sparingly, maybe two or three times a season.'

6:
'Spider in the Web'

Talia hugs Taro Isogi warmly. Her old friend is on Babylon 5 to present a radical new plan for Mars. He has a vision of Mars going independent without bloodshed, trading the planet's resources for the economic support that alien worlds can provide. Amanda Carter of the Mars Business Affairs Committee has her doubts, but agrees to put forward his idea.

Talia and Isogi discuss the plan as they walk through Babylon 5, but are stopped by a man in the corridor. 'Free Mars,' he says and grabs Isogi by the throat with a black, almost-mechanical hand. Sparks crackle across Isogi's face and torso as an electric charge runs through his body. The man pushes Talia aside and she watches as her friend falls lifeless to the ground. The man flinches in pain. A memory flashes across his mind and Talia sees it telepathically. An Earth cruiser fires at him and his ship explodes in a mass of colour and light and sound. She is seeing the moment of his death.

DNA tests on strands of his hair identify him as Abel Horn, a Free Mars terrorist who is officially dead. Sheridan thinks he could be the result of Project Lazarus, an attempt to implant machines in human minds. Early cyber experiments showed that people could not live with machines inside them, so this project took people at the point of death. They were put under almost complete control of a computer intelligence and fixated on the moment of their death to cut out all conscious thought.

Amanda Carter is shocked to see Abel Horn alive

and in her quarters. He has come to ask for help,
but he is gripped by a sudden seizure that sends him
into violent spasms. Before he blacks out he
mentions Talia's name and Amanda sends for her.
Horn grabs Talia as she enters and pleads
desperately: 'You saw it in my head. Tell me what it
means.' The vision flashes across Talia's mind again,
but this time it goes further. She sees an operation.
Doctors stand over him, fitting his mechanical arm,
and standing beside them is a psi cop.

The door opens and Sheridan, Garibaldi and his
team aim their weapons at Horn. 'Mars will never be
free until the sands run red with Earther blood,' says
Horn, grabbing a PPG and firing a shot that
narrowly misses Garibaldi's head. Sheridan returns
fire and hits Horn in the chest. The blast throws him
back against the wall and he sinks to the floor.
'Thanks for ending it, Earther,' he says as death
finally claims him.

An energy surge builds up in his body and
everybody runs out into the corridor. Horn's body
reaches critical and explodes in a violent flash of
white light that sends Sheridan crashing to the floor.
He pulls himself up looking dejected. 'No trace ...
no evidence ...' he says.

Amanda admits that she and Horn were once a
part of the Free Mars movement before it turned to
terrorism. That admission is enough to ruin her
career, but Sheridan promises not to report it if she
agrees to try to push through Isogi's plan for Mars's
independence.

Garibaldi, meanwhile, wants to know how
Sheridan knew about the Lazarus Project. Sheridan
has been investigating rumours of a rogue agency
inside Earthgov called Bureau 13. He thinks they
regarded Isogi as a danger to Earth policy on Mars.

They wanted Horn to destroy Free Mars from the inside, and possibly to ruin Amanda Carter as well. 'There's a spider in the web, Mr Garibaldi,' he says, 'and I intend to find it.'

In Joe Straczynski's original premise for 'Spider in the Web', Talia Winters inadvertently comes into telepathic contact with a murderer and sees a clue in his head which she doesn't understand. That basic story was expanded by the writer and story editor Lawrence G. DiTillio. 'I added all the Mars stuff,' he explains. 'We'd shown the Mars rebellion going on and I said, "I'd like to bring that back because it's kind of an incident that we refer to and let it drop."' And so the murderer became a Free Mars terrorist.

This was the first episode directed by Kevin G. Cremin, the production manager on *Babylon 5*. He knew they were trying to get better-known actors to guest on the show and so he suggested Michael Beck for the role of Abel Horn. 'Michael Beck was a friend of mine,' he says. 'I had worked with him on a CBS movie I produced about a year or so prior to coming to *Babylon 5* and I had talked to him to see if he would be interested. We didn't have an open pocketbook to pay the salaries that a lot of these guys were used to, so as a favour to me he said he would consider it. I pitched the name out there for Joe and John and I seemed to get a good reception. So he came down and I thought he did a really good job.'

There was a lot of discussion over how to portray Abel Horn's biomechanical hand. Larry DiTillio had wanted it to be 'other-worldly', but it simply wasn't possible. 'That was a great idea and we definitely wanted to go with it,' says Kevin Cremin, 'but if we did it CGI with Ron [Thornton, visual effects designer] and the boys, the chances of it being ready to get on the air in the second season were not good. So conceptually we had to go back to something a little more mechanical and try not to see it, other than when it was specifically used to zap the people that Able was intent on zapping. We had a combination of a mechanical hand that had been built by Optic Nerve and then we augmented that with the lightning streaks that Ron Thornton and the guys were able to come up with.'

Abel Horn was nothing but a pawn, forced to relive his death over and over in his mind so he could be controlled by a computer intelligence. He reaches out to Talia Winters, the telepath, who is the only person who can see inside his head. It was a good episode for Talia in the way it both used her telepathic ability and gave her the chance to have a real friend in the shape of Taro Isogi. 'I got to display a warmth that Talia never gets to display,' says the actress Andrea Thompson. 'I should imagine for a telepath it's got to be a very lonely existence because you don't get the same kind of contact that human beings normally get ... She never touches anybody, and of course, there are the gloves. To touch someone would be like me walking into your house and looking in your closet. A touch isn't just a touch, a handshake isn't just a handshake any more, it becomes something much more. And when she's waiting in the room [for him] I wanted to get the sense of anticipation and excitement, almost like a kid before Christmas morning, and then be able to hug him.'

When Isogi is killed, that friendship is violently taken away from her. She has to reach out to someone and that someone is Garibaldi. After a long time of chasing her, at last he seems to be making contact. The actors have a real-life relationship, of course, and this is something Larry DiTillio wanted to exploit. 'At that point Jerry and Andrea were a couple and there was definitely chemistry between them which was usable dramatically,' he says. 'All that was cut out later on because Joe didn't want to go that way. I thought it would be really interesting to have a triangle between Talia, Ivanova and Garibaldi.'

That tender scene between them reveals some of Talia's background as she remembers Abby, the woman who looked after her when she first joined Psi Corps. 'I loved that little scene – it's a beautiful little scene,' says Andrea. 'You see a little bit more about her. I think in the beginning you could have been driven to say, "Isn't it amazing how cold Talia is?" but in the end I wanted to get people to get the idea, "Isn't it amazing that she still has this kind of warmth?"'

It presents a different view of Psi Corps. The Corps really is mother and father for Talia and she remembers that first contact as a warm, safe place. It contrasts with the horrific side of the organisation which is again high-lighted in 'Spider in the Web' with Bureau 13, the agency that put a machine in Abel Horn's mind and killed Isogi with the intention of destroying his plan for Mars. 'Most people think it was a branch of Psi Corps because they saw the psi cop,' says Larry DiTillio. 'It wasn't. It was actually a deep-seated agency within the government that knew what Psi Corps was planning to do and at some point I would have used it to work against Psi Corps. Now, would that have jogged with Joe's plans? I don't know. I wanted to bring a third force in that nobody could be sure what side they were on. Bureau 13 was responsible for Knight 1 and Knight 2 in "And the Sky Full of Stars", Joe's episode, and several other things that involved Sinclair. It was all the work of Bureau 13, which I intended to bring back.'

'There's a point where you begin to hit overload on conspiracies and "Spider in the Web" kind of tipped the scales a little bit in the other direction,' says Joe Straczynski. 'We had enough groups going on as it was. I'm not sure in retrospect if we needed to have one more brought into the game in the form of Bureau 13. But it [the episode] helped to point to Sheridan as a problem solver, as someone who was interested in conspiracies, which validates why he is there in the first place, and shows that there's more going on with him than meets the eye.'

Sheridan's background, as we saw it when he first came aboard the station, was very much that of an ordinary high-ranking soldier. He fought in the Earth/Minbari War and he was the personal choice of President Santiago to head Babylon 5. But over time, the audience's initial perception was gradually manipulated to sense something bubbling under the surface. It wasn't revealed until the eleventh episode, 'All Alone in the Night', and at this stage not even Bruce Boxleitner knew his character had a secret agenda. 'I was given the indication that he did, but I was not told,' says the actor. 'Isn't that fun? Then that keeps me wondering too. I really didn't know, which was kind of enticing because it perks my interest to not know everything. Joe is very clever about that.'

This is also the episode in which we first see Zack Allen, the security guard whose semi-regular appearances eventually earned him a place in the opening titles of the fourth season. It was a very small part in the beginning, but the actor Jeff Conaway was determined to do it. 'I was already a fan of the show,' he says. 'I'd been watching it and I was very excited about the whole deal. I'd gotten another job and it was either this job or the other job and the other job was a much bigger role, but I loved the show so much I didn't care. Then it was in the middle of the shoot that John Copeland came to me and asked me if I would like to do more shows and I said, "Yeah, I'd love to do it." I was really excited and he basically said, "Just be patient because we didn't know we were going to get you so we'll have to figure out something to do with you."' And Zack was there to stay.

7:
'A Race Through Dark Places'

A man, badly beaten, bleeding and bruised lies strapped to a reclining chair with the psi cop Bester leaning over him. He wants to know the route of the underground railway for rogue telepaths, but the man resists. Bester reaches out into his mind and the man struggles in pain. Bester pushes deeper, slowly crushing his mind until the man is dead. 'Doesn't matter,' says Bester with a smile. 'Betrayed by his final thought ... Babylon 5.'

Sheridan is incensed. Earth Central have decided that he and Ivanova have to pay rent on their quarters. He refuses to pay on principle and decides that Ivanova won't pay either.

The rogue telepaths from Downbelow sense Bester is on the station and plan to kill him. But their plans are betrayed by their untrained telepathic thoughts, which float into Bester's mind as they track him and Talia in the Zocolo. 'Get down!' yells Bester as two shots blast across the crowded marketplace and miss. Bester returns fire, and with his trained hand, shoots them dead. Talia escapes down the corridor where she is stopped by some lurkers who inject her with a drug. She falls unconscious and her body is bundled through a door leading to Downbelow.

Talia wakes up with voices swimming through her head. She opens her eyes to see a group of rogue telepaths standing over her. 'We want you to understand,' the leader tells her, and one by one *they tell their stories. Talia listens with tears in her eyes as a woman tells how she refused to marry a P11 to increase the chances of breeding a stronger telepath. She was attacked in her bed and four weeks later she found out she was pregnant. Her baby girl was taken away by the Psi Corps and she never saw her again.*

Sheridan arrives in Downbelow for a meeting with the leader of the underground railway and is surprised to see Franklin step out of the shadows. Sheridan is worried he might scare off the man running the operation, but Franklin doesn't think so. 'I am the guy running the operation,' he says with a smile.

The telepaths sense Bester approaching and Franklin and Sheridan hide. The telepaths join hands and try to use the strength of their combined minds to overpower Bester. But there is a weak link in the chain. Talia. They break contact and Bester fires his PPG, killing the leader. Talia grabs the leader's gun and they both fire, killing rogue telepath after rogue telepath until they all lie dead or dying around them. Bester smiles and leaves.

Sheridan enters the room to find Talia and the rest of the telepaths standing there with their hands linked, still very much alive. Everything Bester believed he saw was an illusion. Sheridan agrees not to report them as the railway leaves Babylon 5. Afterwards, the leader of the telepaths confesses to Talia that their telepathic projection shouldn't have worked. 'You tipped the balance,' he says. 'You're more than you think you are.'

Sheridan informs Ivanova she won't have to sleep on the couch in his office any more. He has solved the rent problem by diverting money set aside for combat readiness. Ivanova heads back to her own

*quarters, but before she can fall asleep, Talia arrives
needing someone to talk to. 'I just wanted to say
you were right and I was wrong about the Corps,'
she says. 'I think we need to re-evaluate our
relationship.' Talia takes off her gloves and her
badge and they sit down together to talk.*

'Oh my God, that one!' says Mira Furlan when she is reminded of the scene in which Delenn and Sheridan go out to dinner. 'I wish that episode had gone a little bit further in some way. We had that little scene in the restaurant and then somehow nothing happens. It seemed like a sketch for something that has never been done to the end, but obviously Joe was not rushing that relationship, so he just sips a little bit of salt and gives us a little finger.'

Bruce Boxleitner was also a little taken aback by the scene. 'That's when we started going, "Oh my God, these lines! Joe! A guy and a girl when they talk ..." And he said, "How do you know how a Minbari is? Maybe they're not as sophisticated as an Earth person would be. Maybe they're different, much more innocent, much more shy, much more childlike". I went, "Yeah, that's probably right".'

It is the first time these characters are brought together in a setting that allows more than a hint that their relationship might be moving onto another level. They relate to each other, not as ambassador and captain, but as people. We see Delenn laugh for the first time, and in her attempt to understand what it is to be human, she even looks less alien. However, the execution of that moment was something Mira Furlan felt owed more to commercial decisions than the reality of an alien's first human meal. 'I had a completely different idea about how the scene should work, my behaviour in that restaurant and even about the dress,' she says. 'How would Delenn know how to dress? How would Delenn know what "sexy" means? She wouldn't know, so she would probably make horrible mistakes ... How should one eat in a restaurant if one has never been to a restaurant or never eaten with a spoon or a fork? I think I actually had chopsticks. What do you do? Do you put them in your hair?'

Instead, the comedy in the episode came from Sheridan's point-blank refusal to pay rent for having larger quarters than standard issue. It may seem a trivial matter to Ivanova, but to Sheridan it is a matter of principle. 'One thing that we try to do with the show is ground it very strongly in reality,' says Joe Straczynski. 'Bureaucracy has a tendency to mess with you in small trivial and mind-bogglingly petty ways and how much more petty can they get than an argument over the square feet in someone's quarters? In a point of fact, after the episode aired, one of the military guys sent me a note saying, "I've been in similar situations, not that they asked me to pay rent, but they asked me to go to smaller quarters to give this to somebody else." What works about the show is that not every episode or every battle is for the state of the galaxy. Sheridan fought over every square inch of his quarters with every bit as much enthusiasm as he would fight against the Shadows.'

Ivanova is press-ganged into sharing that enthusiasm and has to join him in sleeping in Sheridan's office – but on separate chairs, of course. 'Any time you do a scene where you're supposed to be falling asleep, you start to feel very childish and start giggling a lot,' says Claudia Christian. 'You've got a blanket around you and it's the middle of the day and you've got a crew around you and you're pretending to sleep.'

The dramatic focus of the episode is the underground railway bringing rogue telepaths through Babylon 5. The obvious thing would have been to have Ivanova running the operation, a conclusion that even Garibaldi is drawn to. But Joe Straczynski didn't do the obvious thing: he decided to put Franklin in that position. It might have been a surprise for the actor, too, if he had not been fore-warned. 'Joe has a way of casting you in the role and says, "Oh by the way ..." and drops something and you kind of go "hmm",' says Richard Biggs. 'Then in traffic, or at home doing the wash, or in your trailer, you're allowing your imagination to take off. So when you read it in the script you're almost prepared. He does it in such a way that you're not thinking about the exact thing that's going to happen, but he leaves it so that your imagination can explore the different possibilities. That brings a lot more contrast, colours and layers to your performance once you get the words.'

It brings the horror of the Psi Corps into sharp focus, and at the heart of that is Bester. It doesn't matter to him that he killed a telepath in interrogation, as long as he got the information that he wanted. 'The first scene was very interesting,' says Walter Koenig who plays Bester. 'I thought having him be a killer in the first scene was pretty extraordinary and I thought that would probably be his last episode. I'm so conditioned to if you do something really awful you've got to be punished for it, but I under-estimated Joe and the way his mind works.'

Joe Straczynski had wanted to bring back Bester since his success in the first season's 'Mind War'. The charac-ter went on to become even more important to the story, but that idea was very much embryonic at this stage. 'I certainly knew that the Psi Corps was going to become more important and the issue of telepaths was going to become more important,' he says. 'It was useful to have someone there as a recurring reminder of the roles of those institutions and those individuals. Walter also got along with the cast. People responded nicely to his char-acter and he seemed like somebody I definitely wanted to do more with down the road.'

Bester's final scene in that episode has him leaving the customs area as Talia looks on, but just before he turns there is moment of hesitation and doubt on his face. Maybe he realizes he can't scan Talia and maybe he suspects that she is hiding something. 'This was the first time I brought this to Joe's attention,' says Walter. 'I said, "If he's so totally duped that they just get away with it without any opposition, I'm concerned that we will lose the element of threat in this character." So it was my request that, as he leaves, he stops and turns around and looks at her as if he's not buying it entirely.'

This is the episode which finally breaks Talia's loyalty to the Corps. There had been moments when her loyalties were torn, like when she helped Jason Ironheart in 'Mind War', but 'A Race Through Dark Places' is where she is forced to confront the horrors of the organization that she belongs to. For someone who had been in Psi Corps since she was five, going up against Bester was like going against her family. Afterwards, she turns to the one person who might understand – Ivanova.

Talia takes off her gloves and her Psi Corps badge, as if stripping away the barriers between her and Ivanova. Taking off the badge was in the script, taking off the gloves wasn't and the director was reluctant to let the actress film it that way. 'I said, "Call Joe. I really think this is important,"' says Andrea Thompson. 'This is a point as an actor when you have to make a stand and people are standing around going, "Oh Christ, is she difficult, she's holding up shooting, we just all want to go home." And you've got to stand out and say, "No, this is important, everything else I can let go, but I've got to have this." We were going to shoot it both ways because at first we couldn't get hold of Joe, and then right before we rolled he called in and he said "OK". It made me feel so good. It was so gratifying to have been on the same page as Joe, because he's such a brilliant guy that sometimes you can be left with the feeling that you're incredibly stupid. I mean, he's just got so much going on, it's hard to keep up sometimes. I went home exhilarated that day.'

8:
'Soul Mates'

*Londo welcomes his three wives aboard Babylon 5
with a beaming smile. It is the thirtieth anniversary
of his Ascension day and the Emperor has deemed to
give him a gift. Divorce. 'By tomorrow I will choose
one of the three of you to remain my wife, and the
other two will be gone,' he says with a chuckle.*

*Talia Winters is sitting in the Eclipse Café
glancing through the menu when she hears a voice
from the past. She looks up to see Matt Stoner, her
ex-husband. She gets up to leave, but he pulls her
back again. He has come to offer her a way out of
Psi Corps, and she can't disguise the fact that she is
tempted. Stoner was once part of the Corps until
telepathic experiments destroyed his talents. He left
the Corps and their marriage was annulled. Now he
is back to offer her the same treatment. 'You'd be
free,' he says, 'and we could be together.'*

*Londo's wife Mariel enters his quarters dressed in
a negligée. She takes his hands and looks dreamily
into his eyes. 'Londo, I'm not like the others,' she
says softly. 'I have always been giving, passionate ...' But out of the bedroom comes another one of
his wives, Daggair, also dressed for bed and ready to
please Londo. Timov, the third wife, walks in on
them with no intention of participating in Londo's
sexual olympics. He protests that they are merely
expressing their feelings for him. 'I can do that,'
says Timov and slaps Londo hard across the face.*

*All dignitaries on the station attend Londo's
anniversary party, a gigantic celebration with food
and drink and presents. Londo opens the box*

containing his present from Mariel, an ancient Centauri statue. As he looks at it fondly, two darts shoot out from its eyes and strike Londo's forehead. His body shakes and he collapses.

Timov walks into the Medlab where Londo lies dying from the effects of the poison darts. She admits that she has the same blood type as her husband and is prepared to let Dr Franklin perform the blood transfusion that will save him, on condition he is never told. 'I don't think either of us could stand the awkwardness of false gratitude,' she says.

Talia decides not to leave with Matt Stoner, feeling it would be walking away from herself. 'If you took away my talents, I don't know what would be left,' she says. But Stoner looks deep into her eyes and tells her she is coming nevertheless. Her expression gradually turns into a warm smile and she takes his hand. Stoner leads her into the corridor where Garibaldi is waiting. He throws a punch, hits Stoner on the chin and knocks him to the floor. Talia blinks as the control over her mind disappears.

Stoner hasn't left the Psi Corps at all. He is still working undercover for them. The experiments they performed on him didn't destroy his abilities: they transformed them into an empathic power with the ability to control others. He came to Babylon 5 for Talia because their genetic compatibility might be able to produce a new generation of empaths.

Londo says goodbye to his three wives in the customs area, having decided to divorce Daggair and Mariel and stay married to Timov. She has made no pretence of love for him, will never be what he wants her to be and cannot understand why. 'Because,' says Londo, 'with you, I'll always know where I stand.' He kisses her hand and she leaves with a surprised smile on her face.

Londo describes his three wives in 'The War Prayer' as pestilence, famine and death. In 'Soul Mates' we get to see why.

The man who was given the task of creating these three characters was Peter David, who made his *Babylon 5* debut with this script. 'I needed someone who could handle the dialogue between Londo and his three wives,' says Joe Straczynski. 'Londo's a very strong character so they had to come up to that level and be able to fence and parry with him. So I figured I needed someone who is good on dialogue, good on characterization and is nuts! Peter fit the bill on all levels.'

Before setting pen to paper, Peter David watched the movie *The Women* on the advice of *Babylon 5*'s creative consultant Harlan Ellison, which helped him get the feel of the wives' personalities. He then took the notions of famine, pestilence and death and moulded the characters around them. 'Famine was supposed to be represented by Timov in the sense that this is someone who is almost emotionally undernourished,' he says. 'If you spell Timov backwards that's vomit, which the actress Jane Carr didn't realize until halfway through the shooting when somebody pointed it out to her. Pestilence, the concept of Daggair – her name was a slight distortion on dagger as if she would slip it through your ribs. She is disease, she is almost like the disease of the soul, that her soul is so bankrupt and corrupt that she will bend with the breeze. I gave Mariel the most angelic and lovely-sounding name to run counter to her personification, which was death. She's the one you have to watch out for: she's sweet, she's smiling and she'll kill you.'

With those three, it is hardly surprising that Londo wants a divorce. For Peter Jurasik, who plays Londo, one of the highlights of the episode was playing opposite Jane Carr again, having previously worked with her on the comedy show *Dear John* (called *Dear John USA* in the UK). The other highlight was working with John C. Flinn III, who is also *Babylon 5*'s resident director of photography. 'John does such a fabulous job controlling and running our crew and he does it in such a special, easy manner. I don't know how he does it,' says Peter. 'So when he directs an episode, I always want to work three times harder. So when I look back on that show one of my memories is that I feel that I was pushing too hard to make it good for the sake of John Flinn.'

Nevertheless, there was a great deal of fun for Londo in his interaction with his three wives, which comes as welcome relief in a season filled with darker moments for his character. One of the most fun moments for Peter Jurasik was Londo's large anniversary party where he got to act in a room dominated by a large portrait of himself. 'You feel like you're being worshipped!' he jokes. 'They still hang that picture in the prop department to massage my incredibly large ego. I jokingly say that I try to convince my wife to let me bring it home and put it up in my drawing room, but she won't allow it.

'That felt like a wrap or a Christmas party for *B5*,' he adds. 'All of the regulars were together. We got to goof together and have a really good time that night and there were lots of laughs on the set. That was the famous episode where Bruce called into the little link on his hand, "Hi, this is Sinclair!"'

That moment became the crowning glory of the second-season blooper reel, as Bruce Boxleitner did indeed call himself Sinclair instead of Sheridan. 'He knew it right away – of course everybody cracked up!' continues Peter. '[Although first] there was a moment of great horror because that transition from [Michael] O'Hare [who played Sinclair] to Boxleitner was a tough one for all the reasons that I think you're aware of. Bruce is a nice, kind man and so was treading softly on the memory of Michael, and for him to just make that faux pas, that slip-up – it was classic!'

The theme of the episode was relationships. While Londo was in the process of ending a couple of his, Stoner, Talia's ex-husband, was on the scene hoping to restart one. Talia refuses partly because the relationship was arranged by the Corps and never worked out, declining his offer to take away her telepathic powers. And, as if to make the situation abundantly clear, she kisses Garibaldi and walks out of the room. That moment was filmed, but cut in editing. It put a different spin on the scene and Jerry Doyle feels his performance seemed inappropriate as a consequence.

'My delivery to him was based upon what happened with Talia, which you didn't see,' says the actor. 'My delivery would have been much different had the kiss not occurred ... I said it like, "I've got to go because I can't believe what just happened" – and then I go chasing after her and then there's a line where I say to her, "Well now that this investigation's over ..." and she says "Well that's entirely up to you Mr Garibaldi." But that got cut.'

There was certainly a relationship building between these two characters, as it was between the two actors in real life, but Joe Straczynski wasn't sure he wanted to go down that path. 'Jerry was pushing for it, Andrea was pushing for it and Larry [DiTillio, *B5*'s story editor] was pushing for it,' he says. 'I really wasn't sure I wanted Garibaldi to go there. I had other plans for Garibaldi. Part of my brain was saying, "Talia may not be here that long and Garibaldi has already lost one relationship and I don't want to get him involved in another one and have that pulled out from under him, on top of everything else that's going on." I just felt, "Let me hold off on this, let me think about this some more."'

To continue the relationships theme to its extreme, Delenn's problem in this episode is the relationship with her own body. After making her part-human transformation, she found herself all in a tangle over her newly acquired hair. 'I couldn't connect with it when I first read it,' admits the actress Mira Furlan. 'I thought, "It's demystifying Delenn. Delenn shouldn't be ordinary. It's banal, it's underneath her." But then I went to talk to Joe. I talked to the writer, Peter David. We had a lot of discussions and then somehow something clicked in my mind and I thought, "Let me try that from the other angle." And actually it worked very well and it's many people's favourite episode, which is interesting. So I was wrong and I admit it completely. It's just that you have to open it out. It's when people say, "Oh, my character would never say that" – you don't know! Maybe he would or she would in a different situation. You have to find that possibility. Because it's like people, you think you wouldn't do something, and then you do it. We're constantly contradicting ourselves.'

Peter David, in looking for a conclusion to this storyline, wondered how human Delenn had actually become and added the scene where she asks Ivanova about having cramps. Mira hated it. 'I *begged* them to change it,' she says. 'It's like elementary school humour, boys' humour, and nothing funny in it for me.'

To Peter – who shares a house with a wife and three daughters – it was a natural progression of the story already laid down. 'I said, "Oh my God, if she's human, how human is she?" If she thinks having a bad hair day is difficult, how in God's name do you explain menstruation to someone who is alien? That's why I put in the end where she says, "Can you tell me why I've been having these odd cramps?" Joe loved it because it set up all sorts of speculation as to Delenn's biology and put forward the very logical question of "Well, if Delenn is menstruating, does that mean that Delenn is capable of bearing a human child?"'

9:
'The Coming of Shadows'

G'Kar sits uneasily with his hand resting on the knife hidden under his clothes as he and other dignitaries await the arrival of the Centauri Emperor. But as the Emperor approaches the reception, his hand clutches at his chest and he sinks to his knees in pain.

G'Kar is incensed that the Centauri Emperor had the indecency to start dying before he could assassinate him! But all G'Kar's murderous thoughts are wiped away when Dr Franklin enters his quarters with a message from the Emperor: 'He came all the way out here, risked his health, endangered his life, so he could stand beside a Narn in neutral territory and apologize for all the things the Centauri have done to your people.'

With the Emperor close to death, Lord Refa tells Londo that they must do something to put themselves in a strong position back home. Londo remembers Morden's offer to choose a target, and so he chooses Narn Outpost 14, which lies on the edge of Centauri space.

A fleet of Shadow vessels shimmer into existence near Outpost 14, shooting at its orbiting space station with powerful energy beams, slicing it into sections that explode with a flare of brilliant white light. Narn fighters swarm to attack, but their fire power has no effect and the Shadow weapons pick them off one by one. The Shadows gather over a Narn city on the planet and train their energy

*weapons on it before vanishing and allowing
incoming Centauri ships to claim the victory.*

'Mollari!' *cries G'Kar, spotting Londo in the
Zocolo. Londo tries to scurry away, but G'Kar pulls
him back.* 'I am going to buy you a drink,' *he says.
Londo is terrified, but G'Kar sits him down by the
bar and he realizes that his Narn colleague hasn't
yet heard the news. Instead, G'Kar is still buzzing
with the Emperor's message.* 'I've heard something
that makes me think there may be hope for us after
all,' *he says, raising his glass to the Centauri
Emperor. Londo drinks sombrely, knowing that the
moment of hope has already passed.*

*A man comes to Garibaldi carrying a message on
a datacrystal. Garibaldi is stunned to see the
message is from Sinclair. Sinclair tells him that the
messenger is one of a group of Rangers who are
working for him. He asks Garibaldi to give them
every courtesy and cooperation.* 'There's a darkness
coming, Michael,' *he says from the monitor.* 'I wish
I could tell you more, wish I could warn you, but
the others don't think it's time yet ... Stay close to
the Vorlon and watch out for Shadows.'

*G'Kar throws a security guard over his shoulder
and hits two others with the ferocity of rage.*
'Mollari! Mollari!' *he screams and he storms down
the corridor baying for blood. He turns the corner
and is faced with Sheridan and an armed security
team.* 'They'll kill everyone! Don't you understand?'

Sheridan orders G'Kar to stay away from Londo.
'You have to decide what's more important,' *he
says,* 'revenge, or saving the lives of your people.'
*G'Kar hesitates for a moment and then with all his
rage and frustration, bangs his fists against the wall
and slides down to the floor, a pitiful dejected sight.*

Sheridan convenes a meeting of the council. G'Kar

announces that his government has decreed that they will not allow the Centauri to devastate their world as they did in the past. 'Our hope for peace is over,' he says solemnly. 'We are now at war.'

'The Coming of Shadows' is a key moment in *Babylon 5*'s ongoing story. The Shadows begin to show their hand by starting a war on behalf of the Centauri, disturbing the balance of the galaxy. From this moment there is no looking back.

'There was a general memo put out by Joe where he said, "This is our best show, this is the level we should strike for each and every week,"' remembers Peter Jurasik, who plays Londo. 'I – only half jokingly – said to him, "Well that would be great if we got these scripts every week!" The point of my little dig was that it really is a group effort. If we get a great script then everybody feels they are on the money acting-wise. It's hard to do that. To get everybody to click at once is a rare thing. "The Coming of Shadows" really feels like a benchmark for our show because of that. Everybody seemed to hit it right off that week.'

The attack on Outpost 14 is a major event on which the story turns, but, as is always the case on *Babylon 5*, the focus is on the characters and how it affects them. It begins with G'Kar and his plan to kill the Centauri Emperor.

'This is the old G'Kar before his epiphanies and inner transformations, where everything's a black-and-white world,' says the actor Andreas Katsulus. '[He thinks] the Centauri are no good. We have to destroy them. How do we destroy them? Kill their leader. I mean really acting on passionate, patriotic motives. It would be like us deciding in the United States, OK, we've got to destroy [the Iraqi leader] Saddam [Hussein], not with missiles or anything, but the man: go for the man and that leadership that's causing all the problems will be gone – this sort of fundamental black-and-white thinking. That's G'Kar's thinking.'

So when Franklin tells G'Kar that the Emperor had come to Babylon 5 to personally deliver a message of peace to the Narn ambassador, it provokes a contrasting change in G'Kar. 'Suddenly he hears the most unexpected thing and here's the character putting aside these black-and-white attitudes towards things and seeing his arch-enemy doing something of a higher nobility than his own activity,' says Andreas. 'He just takes it in. That reaction is totally important in the character's development.'

It heralds the emergence of the new G'Kar, the G'Kar who is prepared to put aside his thoughts of revenge and embrace the chance for peace. It gives him a new enthusiasm for the future and he takes this to Londo. But it is too late. The Narn outpost has already been attacked.

The series was building to this point from the very first episode where the age-old Narn/Centauri conflict flared up through aggression by the Narn. In 'Midnight on the Firing Line' it was the Narn who attacked a Centauri outpost and Londo's comment that it will ultimately lead to war is a prophecy that is fulfilled here. There is a sense of inevitability about it all, but, as this episode points out, the war is engineered by the people with their fingers on the trigger. It is Londo's decision to order the attack on Outpost 14 and it is a choice he makes with his eyes open. He knows what he is doing because, even as he makes the decision to start a war, he asks for forgiveness from the 'Great Maker'.

'The circumstances that lead to the war could be averted at many different stages,' says Joe Straczynski. 'That moment when Londo and G'Kar are at the Zocolo and G'Kar is buying him a drink, that is a moment of incredible irony and sadness for Londo because he sees

Revelations: *Delenn reveals her half-human/ half-Minbari face*

The Geometry of Shadows: *The techno-mages bring Sheridan a warning of coming darkness*

The Geometry of Shadows: *A Green Drazi prepares to kill his Purple brothers*

A ship from the past arrives in The Long Dark

Dr Franklin gets close to one of his patients in The Long Dark

A Race Through Dark Places: *Bester (Walter Koenig) believes he has destroyed the underground railroad bringing rogue telepaths through Babylon 5*

Sheridan and Delenn wait for the arrival of the Centauri Emperor in The Coming of Shadows

Delenn on her way to see the Grey Council in All Alone in the Night

Sheridan, having been tortured by the Streibs, prepares to fight for his life in All Alone in the Night

Sheridan confronts Londo in the Council Chamber

*Draal (John Shuck) controls the great machine
in* The Long, Twilight Struggle

Comes the Inquisitor: *Sebastian (Wayne Alexander) arrives to test Delenn*

Commander Susan Ivanova (Claudia Christian)

A stunt man straddles fire in Comes the Inquisitor

Delenn and Kosh watch as Sheridan jumps from an exploding shuttle in The Fall of Night

right there in front of him that he had a chance for peace – "I just blew it!" When G'Kar drinks to the Centauri Emperor, that's the basis from which you can build diplomatic relations: you see in Londo's face, "My God, what have I done?" That's one of those episodes where you get the feeling that there is no one putting on the brakes in this show and it's totally out of control. I love those kind of moments.'

'People say they liked that scene and it was a scene like so many I have with Andreas,' says Peter Jurasik. 'He's always bringing new and exciting energy to a scene and you just need to keep your eyes and ears wide open because you just don't know what Andreas is going to bring. People talk about what a wonderful scene it is for both of us, but I felt that I just sat there, eyes wide, ears open and took in what Andreas was doing. He did such an intense energetic take on that scene. We did it about three or four times and each time it was totally different. The take that they eventually took [and used in the episode] I remember so clearly. He attacked the scene with so much energy and enthusiasm, G'Kar did, for embracing Londo, it was really surprising to me. If you look at my reaction – or Londo's reaction – he really looked surprised because, as so often is the case, I was really blown away by Andreas's performance.'

There is a warning of where all this is heading for Londo in his dream. He sees himself standing on Centauri Prime with a fleet of Shadow ships flying overhead, as an old man being crowned Emperor and of his final moments being strangled to death by G'Kar. There is no context to these images. They are just glimpses of the future. But the whole tone is very different from the glory Londo is striving for and that presents the character in an ominous light.

These events, already referred to in 'Midnight on the Firing Line', are continually referenced throughout the series as their meaning begins to surface. This, however, was the first time they were seen and the first time Peter Jurasik got to play at being Emperor. 'My famous five- or six-hour make-up with Greg Funk, our make-up artist,' he says. 'He had a great time. That was like being the canvas for Salvador Dali: he would splash a little colour on my face and then step back four feet, and then splash a little colour on my chin. It was really quite something. The downside of doing a character on a TV series is that you're always playing the same character. I'm always playing Londo and the nice thing about playing him as an old man is it gives you a chance to play a different beat, a different tone for the character.'

On the side of light, this episode sees the introduction of the Rangers and the message from Sinclair. Having lost the character at the beginning of the season, the audience were quite surprised to see him brought back in a cameo. 'I knew the character would come back at some point and I wanted to keep the character alive for viewers,' says Joe Straczynski. 'It's appropriate because the Rangers are under Sinclair's jurisdiction at this point. That's what he did when he was on Minbar, and as the leader of the Rangers who knows Garibaldi, it makes perfect story sense to do that. In fact, we actually had filmed that quite some time before, knowing that it was going to be happening this season.'

The episode was such a success on all levels that it won Best Dramatic Presentation of the Year in the Hugo awards, which are voted on by fans at the World Science Fiction Convention. For Joe Straczynski, it was a validation of everything he and his team had been doing on *Babylon 5*, as well as a personal thrill. 'When they announced *Babylon 5* and I stood up, I thought for a moment, "We're having an earthquake" because there was thunder in the room. It was shaking! I realized the fans were just stomping their feet, clapping their hands and yelling at the top of their lungs. Even people around me, other SF authors who didn't know about the show, were looking around startled, thinking, "What the hell's all this?" That was kind of a shock, the extent of real concern from the fans that we get this thing.'

10:
'GROPOS'

Twenty-five thousand Ground Pounder troops arrive unannounced on Babylon 5, swamping the station with soldiers. They are preparing for a classified mission to crush the civil war on Akdor, led by General Richard Franklin, Dr Stephen Franklin's father.

General Franklin sees to his troops before dropping in to see his son and pretty soon the old arguments come around again. The general thinks his son is healing aliens when he should be healing humans, while Stephen says his father is a murderer. Later, Stephen Franklin tells Ivanova what happened and she urges him to try talking to his father again. 'Tell him what you feel,' she says. 'I didn't and I lost the chance.'

The GROPOS are swarming all over the station and Delenn cannot help but pass by them in the Zocolo. She is only saved from being part of an ugly scene when a feisty marine called Dodger steps in. Within moments, Dodger is punching and kicking her way through the gang until the fight is stopped by the distinctive yell of their sergeant major. He has every intention of putting them in the brig, until Garibaldi asks him to overlook it.

Dodger thanks Garibaldi and asks if he can show her around the station. By the end of the evening they are in his quarters and kissing. But after a few moments, Garibaldi is pulling away, asking her to take it slowly, explaining about his confused and turbulent personal life. 'I'm a Ground Pounder,' she says furiously. 'Today I'm scrubbing latrines,

*tomorrow I might be hip-deep in blood ... In
between I take what I can get to help me remember
I'm alive.' She storms out.*

*There is a sense of reconciliation in the air as
General Franklin enters his son's quarters. Both of
them know that this mission is more dangerous than
the soldiers on the ground have been told. 'I've said
a lot of things to you I shouldn't have,' says
Stephen. 'But I didn't say the one thing I should
have. I love you, Dad.'*

*The Casino is full of troops living it up before
they get shipped out. Lieutenant Warren Keffer has
made friends with two of them, Large who has been
a GROPO for thirty years, and Yang who is just
about to see his first action. In the middle of one of
Keffer's war stories he accidentally knocks the
soldier standing behind him and spills his drink. The
GROPO goes to punch Keffer, who blocks the move
and knocks him to the floor. Another man hits
Keffer over the head and the whole bar erupts. A
woman punches Garibaldi, and Dodger defends him
with a high kick to the woman's chin. Fists and legs
and furniture fly everywhere as troops and station
personnel hit anyone who happens to be next to
them.*

*'ATTTTTEN-HUT!' cries the sergeant major from
the balcony and suddenly everything stops. They
have their orders: it is time to go. Dodger manages
to sneak a quick kiss with Garibaldi before she joins
the rest of the troops. 'You never know what you
missed,' she says.*

*A large crowd has gathered in the Zocolo to
watch the ISN report from Akdor. A number of
people slap Dr Franklin on the back as they hear of
his father's victory, and Stephen smiles proudly.
Then, as the crowd disperses, Garibaldi is handed*

> *the casualty list and his expression falls. Keffer takes*
> *the list from him and looks down at the names. They*
> *are all dead. Dodger, Large, Yang – all of them.*

Jerry Doyle had wanted to get Garibaldi in bed with someone almost from the beginning. He made such a fuss that the story editor Lawrence G. DiTillio decided to give him what he wanted in 'GROPOS'. 'Jerry had been ragging on me from Season One saying, "Londo got to go to bed with a woman before I did!"' says Larry. 'So I wrote it and I went to Jerry and said, "Jerry, this is your moment." Jerry said, "You know, I don't think Garibaldi would go to bed with her." I said "Huh?"'

Jerry Doyle was really angling for a romantic liaison between Garibaldi and Talia. He had just filmed a scene in 'Soul Mates' in which Talia had planted a kiss on him (subsequently cut) and he felt the character was going in a different direction. 'So the script comes along and I screw this girl that comes on the space station and I just say, "No, it doesn't work". They said, "What do you mean it doesn't work?" and I say "Well I'm not going to throw away a potential relationship for the sake of getting laid" ... I just thought it was wrong for the character, I thought it was wrong for the relationship, I thought it was going to give the audience a different look at Garibaldi by saying no.'

The scene was rewritten to present an interesting role reversal whereby the woman is making all the moves and the man is saying no. But Larry was unhappy about having to change it. 'I don't think the scene makes sense. I don't think it's right. I think it was right for him to sleep with her. Then her death would have been much more of a blow to him than it was. That was something that we just didn't agree on.'

'GROPOS' focused on the nature of war by shifting attention away from the officers in charge to the people on the ground. Dodger made a play for Garibaldi because she knew she could be dying on her next mission. The other Ground Pounders express the same emotion in different ways. The scene in which they move on Delenn, ridiculing her for the way she looks, has more to do with their desire to have some fun than any prejudice they might have.

'I had a problem with that scene,' says Mira Furlan. 'Why is she all at once so frightened? Why does she need defence from the outside? She was doing all kinds of stuff. She has all these powers. She can be dangerous. She can take care of herself. Also it was somehow unfinished. I come and I was attacked and I go away.'

The trouble escalates into a massive fight started when Keffer accidentally spills someone's drink. He offers to set the matter straight, but the soldier would rather solve the problem with his fists. As soon as he has thrown the first punch, it is an excuse for everyone else to muscle in.

'The thing I wanted to do, I'll be frank, is a huge big bar-room brawl,' says Larry DiTillio. 'From my youth I had always loved these big bar-room brawls where all these soldiers get together and beat the heck out of each other and walk out bloody and saying what a good time they had. Of course Jim was the perfect man for this because Jim loves action stuff.'

Jim Johnston was the director on the episode and used a variety of steadicam shots, including one of Dodger kicking directly at the camera, to add to the action. 'I rented a few of the old cowboy movies where they broke into these brawls, throwing chairs, going over the bar, and stole a couple of shots from there,' he confesses.

Jim's biggest challenge in 'GROPOS' was making it look like there were 25,000 soldiers on Babylon 5 when all he had was a bunch of extras. 'I had the marines circling,' he says. 'I thought you've seen one marine, you've seen another, so I had them going around in a circle. I had every extra three or four times in almost every scene, but it was the only way to get the feeling. I had, maybe, eighty-five extras and I was supposed to make them look like twenty-five thousand!'

Computer trickery helped him out on some scenes when groups of soldiers were made to look larger than they actually were by sticking separate shots together in post-production. One of those scenes occurs towards the beginning where the lines of regimented soldiers swarming onto the station are in fact the same line of people filmed several times over.

On the flip side of the military life is the hierarchy, represented by General Franklin, Dr Franklin's father. This relationship was inspired by real life, and a conversation between the writer Larry DiTillio and actor Richard Biggs. 'I told him about my family. I told him about my father being in the military and he sat and he listened for about an hour,' says Rick. 'I went home and a couple of weeks later the "GROPOS" script came out. There's a lot of correlation with my personal life with my father and with Franklin and his father so it was really nice to play, especially with Paul Winfield coming in [to play General Richard Franklin], who I'd watched for years as I was growing up.'

The two characters come into conflict after only a few minutes of being in the same room with each other. Their jobs, as Franklin sees it, cannot be more different. One is a healer, the other is a killer. But Rick Biggs senses there is a deeper irony. 'They're the same people,' he says. 'His father got to where he is for the same reason that Dr Franklin is chief medical officer. They're both career men, they're both dedicated to their jobs. So of course there's going to be conflict because they're so much alike. Dr Franklin, I feel, has tried his best to be different than his father, but in fact he's the same.'

So much of Franklin's role in *Babylon 5* is in being the doctor, providing exposition and technical data, that it takes an episode like 'GROPOS' or 'The Long Dark' to reveal more about him as a person. 'I thoroughly enjoy the episodes where [the writer] takes the doctor out of Medlab, which is super-comfortable for the character,' says Rick. 'It's that comfortable that you don't really get to see the interesting qualities because he's on top and he's in control. But you take this character out of the Medlab, out of his job, and you put him in a one-on-one relationship with a family member or with a love interest, when he's out of his element, when he's not in control, and that's when you find this is a very interesting character. You get to see *why* he's interesting when you get to see the relationship with his father.'

General Franklin makes it through to the end of the episode, but the people he sent in to fight at Akdor did not, and that was the whole point of 'GROPOS'. 'The only truth about war is that people die,' says Larry. 'I really wanted to show a bunch of people, get really involved in them and then kill them all. A friend called me up and said, "I never thought you'd kill them all. I thought you'd kill one of them, but to see them all dead at the end was a shock to me. And it was a shock to many people. That was exactly what I was going for. I was looking to put a tear in the audience's eyes because these people we had come to know as friends were dead and they were dead for no really good reason.'

'It is emblematic,' says Joe Straczynski. 'There are not always happy endings on this show and many science fiction or action shows have a pretension to glorify war and that's one thing we're trying to avoid saying on this show. There's nothing particularly glamorous about war. Yes, you can have great heroism and great revelation and importance, but war is nonetheless a terrible thing if people you know are going to get killed. That episode helped to bring that home to viewers and set the stage for down the road in the show, that things may not always go well for characters.'

11:
'All Alone in the Night'

*An alien ship blasts out of hyperspace right on top
of Sheridan and his survey team of Starfuries, with
its guns firing. Sheridan's ship is hit and two of its
wings go spinning off into space. Sheridan ejects, his
cockpit flies away as the engines hit critical, and his
Starfury explodes in a ball of light and debris. An
energy beam extends from the alien ship, grabs hold
of Sheridan's cockpit and reels him in.*

*Delenn stands in a circle of light in the Minbari
Grey Council ship with eight empty circles of light
around her. She has been summoned, but the others
will not stand with her. They have voted to remove
her from the Council. They consider her to be 'alien'
after her transformation. Neroon, a member of the
warrior caste, has taken her place, unbalancing the
make-up of the Grey Council for the first time since
Valen formed it from three members from each of
the worker, warrior and religious castes.*

*Sheridan wakes aboard the alien ship, pinned to a
table by a strange organic membrane. He tries to
wriggle free as a torture instrument descends from
the ceiling, but the membrane holds him tight.*

*A metal bar clangs to the floor and Sheridan – his
face cut and bloody – is released from the table. A
Narn carrying a sword and controlled by an
electronic device on his forehead appears before him.
Sheridan takes the metal bar and blocks each move as
the Narn strikes out with the sword. 'Kill me!' cries
the Narn. 'No!' screams Sheridan and with a blow to
the neck and another to the head knocks him
unconscious and disables the electronic device.*

Sheridan's eyes close in fatigue and he enters a dream. He sees himself in his quarters and turns to see Ivanova, who puts a finger to her lips for him to be quiet. 'Do you know who I am?' she asks. He turns to see another version of himself looking down from the bridge above the Central Corridor. The second Sheridan looks across at Garibaldi, who stands with a white bird on his shoulder. 'The man in between is searching for you,' he says. Sheridan looks back down at the first version of himself, who is now wearing a psi cop uniform. Beside him, Ivanova is wearing a black veil in mourning. 'You are the hand,' she says. He turns and sees Kosh. 'You have always been here,' says the Vorlon, and, with a start, Sheridan wakes up, back in the alien ship.

The Minbari once encountered the aliens who have captured Sheridan. They are the Streibs, a race who examine species to assess their defence capabilities. Delenn gives Ivanova the location of their homeworld and a fleet of ships to go to the rescue. When their battle guns attack the alien ship, Sheridan and the Narn take their chance and lever open the wall of their prison. They manage to get to an escape pod and are picked up by the Earthforce ships.

Back on Babylon 5, Sheridan is relieved to see General Hague waiting for him. Hague activates a small device to jam any bugs in the room and tells him it is time to decide whether he can trust his staff.

Ivanova arrives at Sheridan's quarters and finds herself part of a select invited party consisting of herself, Garibaldi and Franklin. 'Ever since the death of President Santiago, something unpleasant has been going on back home,' Sheridan tells them.

'We have to do something, or risk losing everything we hold dear.' Sheridan looks around at his staff and, one by one, they agree to join him.

Sheridan is forced to fall back on his wits and his own physical strength if he is to stay alive in 'All Alone in the Night'. It takes the captain out of the comfortable environment of Babylon 5 where he is in control and puts him in a situation where he is a pawn in someone else's game. To be tortured for no apparent reason and be made to fight a succession of aliens is a situation that would terrify anyone, and Bruce Boxleitner wanted to convey that in his performance to make it as real as possible. 'They wanted a very heroic Captain Kirk and I wanted to play a very scared, drugged [man],' he says. 'I just wanted to be a little more vulnerable, I guess, and emotional.'

It was a point of discussion for the torture scenes in which Sheridan is strapped to the table by some organic alien material, unable to escape as he watches the torture instrument descend from the ceiling. 'I had no idea what was coming down; that was going to be CGI'd later,' he says. 'They said "It's coming right down, it's going to bore right down there." And I was going, "Holy man, I would try and do anything I could to get out of there", not just stare at it and go "Go on, I dare you", not the typical thing like a cartoon hero, but squirm and scream for help.'

Incidentally, that stuff that strapped him to the table was just as weird in real life as it appeared to be on screen. 'They put it on you and it's kind of wet,' says Bruce. 'Then it hardens, dries on you, it's stretched over you like a membrane.'

The episode allows action to be injected into the storyline. *Babylon 5* is not bereft of action by any means – there had just been a bar-room brawl in 'GROPOS' and a devastating space battle in 'The Coming of Shadows' – but this was different. This was putting Sheridan in a position we hadn't seen him in before. He hasn't got a PPG to hand or Garibaldi's security team waiting around the corner to save him. This is more like a traditional action hero, in hand-to-hand combat with a sword-wielding Narn and only a metal pipe to defend himself with. 'I damn near collapsed because the pipe I used was a real pipe,' says Bruce. 'It was heavier than a baseball bat, much heavier, so a whole day swinging that thing around, my arms were around my feet by the time I went home. By the time I walked out of the door, I couldn't lift my arms I was so sore. We choreographed the fights with Marshall Teague [who played the Narn], who's an adept swordsman. But I wanted them clumsy-looking, not some Errol Flynn, Basil Rathbone foil with sophistication. I wanted stumbling, falling into each other, clubbing type of thing and I think we got that.'

Out of all this came the surprising moment as Sheridan, overcome by exhaustion on the floor of the alien ship, is touched by Kosh. It is the beginning of their relationship and the dream is a key moment in foreshadowing events to come. The filming was very straightforward for Bruce Boxleitner, who had to do little more than stand in the studio and look in certain directions as the camera rolled. It was not so easy for Claudia Christian, who was the one with a raven on her shoulder. 'That bird was going a little bit hyper on us,' she says. 'He was fluttering around and his claws would get caught in my hair. And his wings! You have to stay perfectly still and then they placed him on my shoulder, but his wings were so long it was just like "whhharr!" So I was staying perfectly still the whole time so it wouldn't make the bird even more freaked out. He was a bit nervous, that bird. It wasn't a real pro, I think.'

Jerry Doyle had to act with a dove on his shoulder, but

it was the actor rather than the bird who misbehaved on this occasion. 'It was a nice dove,' he says. 'It was a nice little bird on a string and the bird wrangler [handler] was a nice guy and he was standing off in the corner. I had gone to the prop man and gotten some white feathery material, and the bird was on my shoulder and I had it by the string so it wouldn't fly away. So the guy turned his head and I pulled the bird down and shot out all these feathers and the crew just busted up thinking I'd killed the bird! I guess the bird wrangler didn't think it was too funny – but too bad!'

The theme of being 'all alone in the night' is continued in Delenn's expulsion from the Grey Council. At the beginning of the season, she had embarked on her transformation full of hope. But as time progressed, she found herself isolated from both the humans, who saw her appearance as an insult, and the Minbari who regarded her as no longer one of their species. She is finally rejected by the Grey Council, the very people who understood the prophecy and were most likely to support her.

The person who remains at her side throughout this is Lennier. He remains loyal even though the disfavour shown to Delenn may reflect on him, and there is a sense that something deeper is going on in this relationship. 'I went to Joe early in the second season and I said, "I think Lennier is in love with Delenn,"' says Bill Mumy who plays Lennier. 'He was really taken back by that. I said, "Let me explain. I'm not saying this so there's a make-out scene. I don't think Lennier would make a move on Delenn – I don't think he would physically go for her out of respect for her – but I think underneath it all he's really in love with her, much more so than just dedicated to her." He said, "Let me think about that." So he went away, and came back and said, "Yeah, I like that a lot. Let's do that, but keep it subtle." So I started playing Lennier that way very early on in the second season.'

The episode ends by taking an unexpected turn when Sheridan is revealed to have been spying on his staff. It was all prepared for nicely by the arrival of General Hague, but the audience was far too concerned about what was happening to Sheridan in the Streibs' ship to worry about Hague. Then Sheridan is rescued and what Hague has to say puts the rest of the episode in the shade. 'I love doing that to viewers,' says Joe Straczynski with glee. 'They think, "Oh great, I can sit back, the worst is over now" and then I sneak up behind them with a baseball bat and hit them really hard. Actually, I was at a fan gathering in Chicago and saw that episode with a bunch of fans who were seeing it for the first time and you could hear a pin drop at that point. They completely did not see it coming. I blind-sided them totally and they were just stunned, which was exactly the reaction that I wanted.'

Sheridan's character suddenly becomes twice as intriguing at this point and one might ask why Joe waited so long to increase interest in the new captain. 'It's the same thing that we did with Londo,' he says. 'I know that because Bruce has a reputation for doing light dramatic or light adventure kinds of roles that when he came on board – particularly with the smiling attitude and asking about fresh fruit – that people would come to assume that that's all the character was. I like to get people comfortable with that notion, like I did with Londo, then yank their blanket. This was the episode where I begin this process, saying, "You think you know this character, but you don't. There are depths here that you haven't seen yet." That really was the moment to do that. If I had set it up at the beginning you wouldn't have had the moment of "Oh my gosh, look at that".'

12:
'Acts of Sacrifice'

G'Kar watches as Centauri fighters fire at a fleeing Narn transport carrying seven hundred young and female Narns. A Narn cruiser moves in to take the brunt of the Centauri assault and the transport escapes through a jump point. The Centauri continue to fire at the Narn cruiser until the whole vessel is one giant, exploding mass of light. G'Kar turns off the replay of the battle and faces Sheridan. He begs for Earth to intervene in the war.

Two representatives of the Lumarti have arrived on Babylon 5 and Ivanova has been given the task of making sure they sign on. The Lumarti see themselves as a superior species and will not lift a finger to help anyone lower down the evolutionary ladder. They are unimpressed with the station until they see the unfortunate lurkers scratching out an existence in Downbelow. They think it is an inspired way of isolating the inferior members of society. Ivanova tries to explain their misunderstanding, but they will not hear of it. The head Lumarti, Correlilmerzon, agrees to conclude the deal to join Babylon 5 – after he and Ivanova have had sex!

Skirmishes between Narns and Centauri are erupting all over the station. G'Kar angrily tells the other Narns they are jeopardizing their chances of forming an alliance with other races. But they are baying for blood and stab a Centauri to death as a message to their opponents.

Londo catches up with Garibaldi in the Casino in the hope that his 'good, close friend' will stay and have a drink. Garibaldi is busy and reluctantly says he may stop by later. Londo stays until he is the last solitary figure at the bar and the staff are cleaning up around him, but Garibaldi doesn't show.

G'Kar joins a group of Narns as they make preparations to kill every Centauri on the station. G'Kar accuses the leader of the group of attempting to take away his authority, something that can only be done by force. The Narn leader rises to the challenge and kicks G'Kar on the chin. G'Kar grabs his head and kicks him in the face. The Narn pulls a knife and slashes at G'Kar. G'Kar jumps back and then kicks, punches and wrestles until a final blow to his opponent casts him painfully to the floor. 'This ends now!' he cries at the crowd of Narns. 'If peace on this station is the only way to win the war at home, then peace we will give them.'

Sheridan and Delenn call G'Kar to a secret meeting. Neither Earth nor Minbar will give him military aid, but they can help to save lives. Minbari ships will deliver food and medical supplies to neutral territory and smuggle out Narns by return. G'Kar thanks them and leaves the room, not knowing whether to laugh or cry at what little he has achieved.

Ivanova poses evocatively by the doorway to her bedroom, ready for sex. She dances round the Lumarti chanting and shouting in a cross between a child's game and a fake orgasm. 'Boom-shob-a-lobba ... Yes! Yes! Yes! Yeeees!' she screams. Correlilmerzon looks bemused, but why should he know how humans really have sex?

Londo agrees that, in order not to provoke more trouble, he will not press for a trial of the Narn that killed the Centauri. Sheridan and Garibaldi are stunned at Londo's compromise and later Garibaldi

> *joins him at the bar for that promised drink. 'It is*
> *good to have friends, is it not Mr Garibaldi?' Londo*
> *reflects. 'Even if it may be only for a little while.'*

The theme of acts of sacrifice plays throughout this episode as each character has to sacrifice something in order to achieve their goal. For Ivanova, it is the sacrifice of her dignity to get the Lumarti to agree to support Babylon 5. 'I asked Joe Straczynski to write me a comedy scene,' says the actress Claudia Christian. 'I just didn't expect "boom shuck-a-lucka-lucka" with the Lumarti.'

Joe remembers that initial conversation very well. 'I said, "Are you sure you want to make that request?" and she said yes. So I began to think of ways to resolve the Lumarti situation with some comedy. She wants funny, I gave her funny. That's the first rule on this show: be careful what you ask for because I will give it to you and it may not be exactly what you had in mind.'

'I didn't expect that at all,' continues Claudia. 'I'm like, "Sorry I asked!" I asked for some comic relief for the character because – Jesus! – her mother dies, her father dies, her brother's dead, she's Russian, she's Jewish, she's uptight, she's militaristic, she's disciplined. Give her a little levity! So he comes up with "boom-shuck-a-lucka-lucka boom", that whole thing with the Lumarti. He wrote it, I performed it and that's where it lies. But I had a good time doing it. It was fun and the fans love it.'

The script called for Ivanova to dance around the unsuspecting alien, but the exact choreography was open to interpretation. The director, Jim Johnston, remembers there was a lot of head-scratching about that one. 'Claudia and I didn't know exactly what to do with this,' he says. 'So we had several discussions over how we were going to pull this off, and that's what we came up with. I said, "Maybe we should just do a figurative dance around this whole idea of sex and we'll just con-fuse him." So that became the dance that we created and he took it that that was the way humans did sex. It took us a long time to get there because we had a few ideas how to do it, but this seemed to be so much fun, and that's what we decided it should be – fun.'

There was a much more serious side to the Lumarti in their attitude towards other races. It is possible to see the logic in their wholehearted subscription to the theory of evolution, that the laws of nature should be allowed to follow their course without interference. But it is a twisted logic. When Ivanova takes them into Downbelow, it is clearly an embarrassment for her to have to show another race that humanity is not able to cope with its homeless people. The Lumarti's attitude that it is a good thing for humans to be living like this is clearly shocking to her. It is an abhorrent attitude and one that is probably best expressed when Dr Franklin takes an extreme example and says they would not even lift a finger to save another's life.

'What I was trying to do with that was look at the approaches we have now in society which say "Well, let the poor fend for themselves",' says Joe. 'The "we don't interfere with lesser races" [rule] seems a very arrogant, mean-spirited rule to me. I think if someone is in pain, it doesn't matter where they're coming from, the person's in pain, you do what you can to help. And we become, in many ways, "leave the other guy alone, sod him, do what you can for yourself" and I wanted to take that to the ulti-mate extreme and put that in people's faces.'

The sacrifice for Londo is compromising on a trial for the Narn who confessed to murdering a Centauri on the station. On the surface, his reasons for doing it are to help prevent trouble, but there is a more personal reason why he decides to do a favour for Sheridan and Garibaldi. This is a Londo who should be revelling in victory, flush from the success of the Centauri attack and his rise in prestige back home. Instead, he is alone. Other Centauri only want to know him because he now has influence which he can use in their favour. Aliens want to avoid him because he represents the force that has disrupted peace in the galaxy. Even Garibaldi is reluctant to take a 'chemically inoffensive' drink with him. Londo is so desperate for a friend that he hangs on at the bar waiting for Garibaldi to join him, long after everyone else has gone home.

'In order to get Londo into a place where he became truly tragic, Joe needed to make him aware of his mistakes and what the problems of his actions were,' explains Peter Jurasik. 'That was one of his initial steps to make him do that, get him alone and pull people away from him. When we first met Londo in the pilot and during the first season, one of the things that kept you interested – if you were interested in the character at all – was that he was this fun-loving guy who you'd want at your company party, and for Joe to void him of all that and to pull all that out from under him was important to do in the second season in order to get to a place where he can really start to see his mistakes and start to understand them. Joe did that in this episode by making him feel lonely and finally pulling Garibaldi away.'

Londo is beginning to face the consequences of his actions, while G'Kar is beginning to act on the lessons he learned. In 'The Coming of Shadows', Sheridan stopped him from killing Londo in revenge, and in 'Acts of Sacrifice' G'Kar must do the same for a group of Narns on the station. Their lust for blood is reflected in his own heart, but he knows that help from the other races is vital if they are going to make a stand against the Centauri. Going on a killing spree will only destroy their chances of that. They have to sacrifice their immediate satisfaction for the future good of their people.

This is the new G'Kar, following the impulses of his head and not his heart, but he does so with the same passion and conviction as always. He puts his life on the line when he makes a stand against the Narn rebel leader and the consequences could have been much worse had the knife laced with Drazi poison cut deeper into his flesh. He may have chosen the path of the diplomat and not the warrior, but he retains his pride and walks tall after being injured in the fight, careful not to show weakness.

He hoped it would bring him military aid from the other races, but all Delenn and Sheridan can offer is second-hand food, medical supplies and an escape route for refugees. 'He doesn't know whether to laugh or cry because he has gained support, but it's a drop in the ocean to what he needs,' says the actor Andreas Katsulus. 'I totally understand why Joe wrote that direction. He goes in the hallway and he doesn't know whether he's won or lost at that minute. He has both emotions clanging with each other inside of him. He's restrained every impulse he had to shout and fight. He said, "Yes, OK, if that's all you can do for me."[And he's thinking] "I mustn't lose this because I risk losing even this support if I throw a tantrum right now and really start cursing them out and putting them down. All hope is lost for the aim that I set for myself. I've gained it but – oh my God! – it's cost me inside". Big stuff. Joe is cruel to make actors go through these things.'

G'Kar proved that his way was the right way, that in stopping the violence he was able to gain some help from the Earthers and the Minbari. But the irony is that the aid comes on condition of secrecy and he cannot tell the other Narn at the risk of losing it. It means they will still need convincing of his ability to lead them and his battles are not over.

13:
'Hunter, Prey'

Dr Jacobs approaches a stallholder in Downbelow
and, in hushed tones, asks about getting a fake
identicard. The stallholder senses the desperation in
his voice and refuses, knowing it means trouble. The
stallholder is right: Dr Jacobs was President Clark's
personal physician and now he is on the run with
information that could blow the Earth Alliance
apart.

As Babylon 5 security search the station for the
rogue doctor, a woman brings Sheridan a message
from General Hague. The information Jacobs is
carrying is evidence that Clark lied when he said he
had a 'virus' that stopped him being on board his
predecessor's ship when it exploded. It could help
prove Clark was behind Santiago's assassination.

Franklin trained under Jacobs at Harvard, which,
Garibaldi knows, gives them an advantage if they
are going to find him before their own security
teams. It means going into Downbelow to find him
and Garibaldi dons a wide-brimmed hat as a
disguise. 'Why is my life suddenly passing in front of
my eyes?' says Franklin to himself.

Jacobs emerges nervously out of a transport tube
in Downbelow where a man – Max – blocks his
path. Jacobs looks out of place in the dark and
dismal surroundings and Max knows it. He rips
open the lining of Jacobs's jacket and finds a
datacrystal hidden in a secret pocket. He realizes his
hostage could be worth a great deal of money.

Sheridan asks Kosh if they could try to
understand each other a little better. It was Kosh

who recently entered his dream, after all. Kosh says Sheridan is not ready to understand a Vorlon when he does not even understand himself, but agrees to teach him 'until you are ready … to fight legends''.

Max's henchman answers a bang on the door in their little corner of Downbelow to find Garibaldi sticking a PPG in his face. He slams him down against a table where the man grabs a screwdriver and lashes out at Garibaldi, stabbing him in the arm. Garibaldi reels in pain, while Franklin finds a fighting instinct from somewhere and kicks and punches the man until he falls to the floor. They untie Jacobs, but Max isn't there and he is the one with the all-important datacrystal.

Garibaldi is waiting for Max when he comes back and demands the datacrystal, firing his PPG into the wall. Max protests that he doesn't know what he is talking about, so Garibaldi fires again, this time a little closer. 'I'm in a really bad mood,' he says. Max tenses as another PPG blast whizzes past his head. 'Now, give me the fragging datacrystal or I'm going to start getting surly!' Garibaldi points his gun point-blank at Max, who steadily reaches into his pocket and pulls out the datacrystal.

Earth Special Intelligence orders Sheridan to use internal scanners to detect the coded identification crystal injected into all presidential staff, including Jacobs. They need to get him off the station, and there is only one docking bay unguarded.

After the internal scanners show no sign of Jacobs, Sheridan, Ivanova, Garibaldi and Franklin gather at Docking Bay 13 where Kosh's ship has just returned and is waiting for them. An opening appears in its shifting, green, organic surface and a tentacle-like arm reaches out from inside, depositing a cocoon at their feet. The skin of the cocoon fades

*away to reveal Dr Jacobs inside. The doctor wakes
and stares back at the ship that had protected him.
'While I was asleep ... the ship ... it sang to me,' he
says with wide, enchanted eyes.*

Babylon 5 is full of images of spaceships, but here the
focus is on Kosh's ship, which is more than a device
for travelling to the stars — it is an object of wonder. It is
just as mysterious as its master, with a skin of mottled
green shifting patterns that hide Vorlon secrets underneath. It is organic technology far in advance of human
experience, and as alive as any alien creature, at least as
far as the scanners on Babylon 5 can tell. Simply being
near it or inside it can affect you, as the maintenance
crews of Docking Bay 13 and Dr Jacobs found out. 'It's
that sense of wonder in the show that technology's not
just machines and equations,' says Joe Straczynski. 'The
whole notion of if you spent too much time with it, you'll
be having strange dreams and it sings to you — these are
things that you don't normally associate with ships. It has
that lyrical quality about it, and I like that part of it a lot.'

We had seen Vorlon ships before, of course, but this
was the first time the characters took time to consider
what they were looking at. The gigantic splendour of the
craft was, as always, created in post-production, meaning the reality of filming the scene for the cast was
staring in wonder at a blue screen. 'They described to me
that it moves, that it breathes,' remembers Bruce
Boxleitner, who plays Sheridan. 'That's where the
theatricality of this comes in, where you have to imagine.
You would have to do the same thing on the stage,
imagining for the audience. You have to try and convey
that awe ... I think Sheridan has always been fascinated
by the alien races. That's part of the reasons why he
went out and joined Earthforce. I think I've said that in
certain scenes, always wanting to know what's on the

other side, what other world is over there. So he has a very childlike, boylike fascination with the new technology and especially with the Vorlons which we've heard so much about and had so little contact with.'

The first suggestion of a link between Sheridan and Kosh came when the Vorlon touched his mind in 'All Alone in the Night'. The matter is pursued here when Sheridan makes an effort to talk to him. It is the beginning of a growing relationship, but it is Kosh who is control. When Sheridan asks, 'What do you want?' – echoing Morden's question from 'Signs and Portents' – Kosh teaches Sheridan to ask the Vorlon question instead, 'Who am I?'

It begins another journey for Babylon 5's command staff as they begin to take a stand against the Earth authorities. For Garibaldi and Franklin, it involves going undercover to Downbelow, and – particularly for Franklin – taking them out of his natural environment and placing them somewhere where they feel uncomfortable. 'I think that's when you get to laugh at Franklin, to see this doctor in a situation where he's going to be physical, he's in danger,' says the actor Richard Biggs. 'When you see Dr Franklin in the Medlab, he's not in danger, he's trying to save lives. But now I'm in physical danger and that's when the humour came out. He's in way over his head. Garibaldi is at ease: he does this for a living and he's got this doctor tagging along who's constantly saying, "What am I doing here?"'

Even for Garibaldi, he doesn't have the backup of his security team, and he doesn't have the symbolic protection of his Earthforce uniform. It doesn't all run smoothly for him, either, because he gets stabbed by one of Dr Jacobs's captors. That incident gave Jerry Doyle a few doubts when he first read the script. 'It's the way some of this stuff is written,' he says. 'Franklin's in my quarters and I'm putting a gun behind my belt, a gun in my left leg, a gun in my right leg, a bazooka in the back of my pants,

I've got an atom bomb under my hat, I've got a flak jacket on and I end up getting stabbed with a screwdriver! It's like, come on! I feel neutered here! The way it was blocked, [I thought], "This is really going to look kinda silly", but they got it all figured out like he did catch me off guard and I got stabbed.'

It produced some nice interplay between the two characters. They even stopped to take stock at one moment, allowing Franklin to have a thoughtful speech about how the future looked so bright when he was twenty-two and how it turned out not to be that way. 'I think it's a feeling that we all have,' says Joe Straczynski. 'It's a theme that I've been beating upon for a long time. There was a time as a kid when I remember we were all fascinated by the future. I remember they built kitchens of the future and cars of the future and it was something that was talked about every day: what it was going to be like, when it was going to get here. Somewhere along the way we kind of lost that fascination with it, and I wanted to address that. The future ain't what it used to be.'

'It spoke to me too,' says Rick Biggs. 'There are many times when I read this stuff and I think Joe is specifically pointing things out in my life. He knows that I am thinking these things and he's going to write it for me. It's a beautiful monologue and the way he wrote it touches everyone.'

Jerry Doyle also remembers that scene, but for a completely different reason. 'The candy bar episode,' he says with disdain. 'Couldn't get the goddamn candy bars out of the wrappers. I swear they glued them in there because they were already cut open and all you had to do was take them and shake them out, have them in your hand and you could finish talking. And I'm sitting shaking it and it was like, "Open up, goddamn it!"'

The character of Dr Jacobs says a lot about the growing opposition to President Clark back on Earth and the growing realization about his role in the assassination of President Santiago. Jacobs is a man who is high up in the presidential staff and is prepared to risk everything to bring the information out to prove it. He has no experience of being on the run, and his clothes and his manner make him an obvious target in a place like Downbelow. He can't even ask about buying an identicard without raising suspicion. He is not a young man and the messages he records for 'Mary', who is possibly his wife, give him a vulnerable edge that invites the audience to sympathize with him. For Joe Straczynski, he was just the right person for the story.

'I liked that he was a fish out of water, that he was from a much higher income level and stratum of society, caught up in this awful situation,' he says. 'You have to understand the way I deal with the characters. It's not very conscious in most cases. I create the character and then I kind of know where that person is in the story and I peek in on him and see what he is doing. They kind of have their own life to them after a while. The best comparison I can give is: imagine your best friend walking across the room in the dead of midnight and banging his shin on the coffee table. Now, you know your friend and you know what your friend's going to say when that happens. It's not a question of deciding what your friend will say: it's a question of knowing your friend and knowing what they will say. When I put the doctor in that situation, that's what you begin to do. It sounds kinda weird, but that's how it works.'

The matter is concluded for the staff of Babylon 5 when Sheridan hands over the datacrystal to his contact, who responds by saying, "Until the next time ..." They have, as she puts it, scored a victory for "the good guys", but it is only one battle in a long war. And that is the thought we are left with as the credits roll.

14:
'There all the Honor Lies'

'Hey you!' cries Sheridan at a man who has just stolen his link. Sheridan gives chase down the corridor and collides with a Minbari coming the other way. He apologizes, but the Minbari kicks him and throws him to the floor. Sheridan finds a PPG beside him, picks it up and aims it at his attacker. 'Death first,' says the Minbari and reaches to his side. Sheridan fires and kills him.

The attack was witnessed by another Minbari, but he contradicts Sheridan's story. He says the dead Minbari actually said 'deh fers't' which, in his own tongue, means 'I yield to your authority'. Sheridan accuses him of lying, but the Minbari do not lie as a matter of honour.

Vir is staring dismally into his second drink of the day. He has received notice from Centauri Prime that he is to be replaced as Londo's ambassadorial aide. Londo offers to put in a good word for him, but Vir doesn't know whether he wants to go back home to his family, who do not want him, or stay with Londo and his terrible secrets. 'I'm caught between fire and flood, and if there's a way out, I sure don't see it,' he says.

Londo's attention is caught by a table of laughing Centauri women. He walks over hoping to share the joke, and then sees they are laughing at a doll. It looks just like him.

'It's a mockery!' Londo protests at Sheridan and Ivanova. In order to put off a major diplomatic *incident, they agree to have the dolls removed from Babylon 5's newly created merchandising store. Sheridan mentions his other problem as Londo is about to leave and Londo is surprised to hear him say that Minbari don't lie. Once, he says, a certain Minbari lied in order to save him from embarrassment. 'Apparently, there is honour in helping another save face.'*

Lennier calls the Minbari witness to his quarters, where he tells Lennier the whole incident was a set-up by their Chudomo clan to remove Sheridan ('Starkiller') from running the station. He lied to conceal the conspiracy and thereby maintain the honour of his clan. At that moment, Sheridan and the others emerge from the back and reveal that they have surreptitiously recorded his confession.

Now that the truth is out, Lennier's clan faces dishonour. Sheridan offers a compromise. He suggests that if the witness issues a statement saying what he actually saw without mentioning the background details, it will both save Sheridan and the honour of Chudomo.

Londo tells Vir his replacement has arrived and it is time to pack. Vir is about to return to his quarters, but Londo calls him back and asks him to pack up his stuff. 'I informed Homeworld that, if you were leaving, then I was leaving with you,' he says. Londo has been singing Vir's praises and they have agreed that he can stay.

Sheridan stops Ivanova in the corridor. She seems to be carrying a teddy bear. He smiles at the cute inscription on the back of its baseball shirt, 'Babearlon 5'. Then frowns when he sees the initials on the front, 'JS' for John Sheridan. He demands that the whole merchandise store is 'yanked out, boxed up and shipped out'.

Later, Keffer is flying his Starfury close to Babylon 5 searching for a reported unidentified object when, suddenly, he hears a thump. He looks up to see a cute teddy bear lying flat against the windscreen. He watches it as it slides up the glass and away into space.

When Peter David visited the set of *Babylon 5* to watch his first episode, 'Soul Mates', being filmed he was invited to pitch other story ideas with a view to writing a second episode. Out of his pitch came 'There All the Honor Lies'. 'Originally I saw it as Garibaldi who shoots the Minbari,' he says. 'It seemed logical to me because he is the security chief, but Joe suggested it be Sheridan because of Sheridan's history with the Minbari. So I said "fine". What am I going to do, say "It's my way or the highway"?'

While it extenuates the Minbari's resentment of Sheridan's position because of his actions during the war, it strengthens our awareness of Delenn's belief in him. She believes his version of events, even when the weight of evidence suggests otherwise. She has a conviction that he is destined for a greater purpose, a theme which is constantly foreshadowed throughout the second season, and paid off in 'The Fall of Night'. Lennier follows her lead and, even though it could mean disgrace for his clan, he conspires to prove Sheridan's innocence.

'The show ended way too *Columbo*-ish for me,' says Bill Mumy, who plays Lennier. 'It ended with everybody's hiding in there and taping his conversation and busting him and all that. It was nice that we didn't actually break the clan down with it, but, to me, it ended a bit too "TV".'

One of the people hiding in the back listening to Lennier getting the truth out of the Minbari witness was the lawyer, played by Julie Caitlin Brown, who is better known to *Babylon 5* as G'Kar's aide Na'Toth from the first season. She walked into the story when Sheridan was accused of murder and then more or less disappeared until this moment. It was originally planned to use her to fuse the two threads of the episode together by becoming instrumental in closing down the Babylon 5 souvenir shop.

'My original concept with how we dispense with the souvenir shop is that, in the course of my story, the souvenir shop ends up posing a threat to station security,' explains the writer, Peter David. 'Someone ended up buying a fake PPG there and almost ended up having their head blown off as a result. At the end I had Ivanova working with the lawyer character to file suits with Earthforce to get this thing off the station.'

This was changed when Joe Straczynski wrote the teddy bear into the story. The bear had been a gift from Peter David's wife to thank him for asking her husband to write for the show. She had a little shirt made for it with 'Babearlon 5' written on the back and his initials, JS, embroidered on the front. However, Joe wasn't impressed. 'I hate cute,' he explains. 'I just won't allow it near me.'

'I didn't know Joe wasn't into cute!' protests Peter David. 'I said, "Oh, gee, I'm sorry, send it back, and he said, "No, I will get you for this" and I said "Get me for *what*?"'

Joe subsequently wrote the scenes in which Sheridan takes a dislike to the bear and throws it into space. 'Well!' exclaims Peter, 'when your wife's gift is dissed on national television, retaliation is in order!'

'He retaliated by sticking that bear into his series *Space Cases*,' says Joe. 'They find that bear floating in space and say, "What kind of monster would space a bear?" And it was planted by the evil Straczyn, a race who wants to conquer the galaxy but doesn't have the budget for it!'

Since the souvenir shop no longer posed a threat to station security, it was just a chance to have some fun, particularly with Londo's horror at discovering the shop is selling little effigies of him. 'The prop department made three or four of them,' says Peter Jurasik, who plays Londo. 'At the end of the episode Kurt Phillips, our terrific prop man, said to me, "Peter, would you like a Londo doll to take home and keep?" I'm not one for hanging on to memories and stuff like that and [I turned him down]. I mentioned it to my wife when I got home and she said, "Oh, you should have taken a Londo doll." The next day I said to Kurt, "You know, Kurt, I've changed my mind: I think I *would* like a Londo," and he said, "No, they're all gone. We're now selling them for a hundred dollars apiece"! There was no way for me to get one, so I missed the beat on that, didn't I?'

There was more comedy with Vir, who gets drunk and experiences his first hangover. 'Playing drunk is one of the more difficult things you can do,' says the actor Stephen Furst. 'The key to playing drunk is to try and not to act drunk. Nobody wants to act drunk when they're drunk: they want to hide the fact that they are drunk, or they're just not aware of it.'

It produced a small, but memorable scene where Vir bumps into Talia Winters in the Zocolo and spills his drink. 'I love that scene,' he says. 'That's one of my favourites because his mind is just all over the place. He goes to brush her off and realizes he's touching her. It was all in the script, but my interpretation was a lot more bumbling than was written.'

Vir was often seen as the bumbling aide, but in 'There All the Honor Lies', we catch a glimpse of the person behind that bumbling exterior. It is the first time that things are told from Vir's perspective. He says that Londo's secrets make him feel like he is falling into a pit with no way out, but his loyalty clearly transcends that.

Despite their differences in opinion, their relationship has become very close and so, when Centauri Prime decides to replace Vir, it is Londo who steps in to save him. 'It's the kind of love that can come through a long-term relationship,' explains Peter Jurasik. 'It started out that all Londo was doing was yelling at Vir – he was on his nerves and driving him totally crazy. But over spending a lot of time together, they have not only got to like each other, but to become friends and openly, I think, without overstating it, fallen in love a little bit with each other and really count on each other.'

The relationship between Kosh and Sheridan takes another step forward in this episode when Kosh teaches him 'one moment of perfect beauty'. The soft moving pattern of robed figures, to the accompaniment of a calming Gregorian chant, was achieved with people on wheeled platforms covered in sheets that were delicately lit, and the ceiling was made very low on purpose to intensify the feeling of Sheridan's being humbled. 'That was just sheer fun,' says Bruce Boxleitner. 'Like when you were a child and took all these moving van boxes and built forts with them and crawl through there. I'm six foot three. I had to crawl through this thing and sit down and everything was an effort, and there's this mysterious hooded figure. I knew nothing of what this was about; not that I didn't understand the material – I didn't *have* to understand it: this is all discovery.'

It was a scene that Joe Straczynski added into the story. 'The script was very good, although it was somewhat on the prosaic side and I wanted to take a moment to elevate it slightly,' he says. 'I also wanted to begin the process of Sheridan letting go of certain things [which he does] in the scene where he removes his stat bar, the only thing he has. It's both literal and emotional for him. It's what he holds onto. Letting go of that – and since particularly in that same episode he is in peril of losing his command – it ties in thematically with that episode and with the larger theme of the show with letting go of the command of his position with Earthforce. We see that again in the first episode of the fourth season when his stat bar drops off, signifying a change in him. I love lyrical, magical kinds of moments and that is definitely one.'

15:
'And Now for a Word'

An ISN logo appears on the screen with a flourish of
music and pulls away to reveal a woman sitting in a
TV news studio. 'Good evening, I'm Cynthia
Torqueman. An ISN crew and I recently spent
thirty-six hours aboard Babylon 5 asking hard
questions and, on occasion, getting in a little over
our heads.'

The image cuts to the view from an Earth
transport, looking out at Babylon 5 surrounded by
incoming and outgoing traffic. A Narn ship breaks
away and heads towards a Centauri transport. The
comm link fills with protests from Babylon control
and cries from the Narn captain as the Narn ship
shoots at the Centauri transport and blows it to
pieces.

Cynthia returns after the break, talking to the
camera as she walks through Babylon 5's docking
bay with chaos continuing all around her. Dr
Franklin – brushing off Cynthia's attempts to
interview him – makes on-the-spot evaluations as
patients are wheeled by on their way to Medlab.

Cynthia leads the camera crew into the council
chambers where the Narn's ambassador G'Kar is
addressing the other ambassadors and the League of
Non-Aligned Worlds. 'An inspection of the
destroyed Centauri has found conclusive proof that
she was carrying fusion bombs and support
equipment for ion cannons, mass drivers and heavy-
energy weapons!' Sheridan bangs his gavel as the
place rises into uproar. The camera swings round to
the Centauri's ambassador Londo as he gets to his

feet. 'Our ships have the right to carry any cargo they choose,' he demands. 'We will not surrender our sovereign rights!' Without warning, a shockwave rocks the chamber and the lights flicker on and off. Commander Ivanova appears on one of the monitors. 'Captain, we need you in C and C. We've got a shooting war going on out here!'

A cut to B5's external cameras as a Narn vessel swoops past, firing at the fleeing Centauri ship ahead of it. A stray shot hits the camera and the image turns to static.

Cut to Cynthia in C and C as Sheridan sends a message to the Centauri cruiser. The camera swings round and zooms in on him. 'Any hostile action taken by you against ships entering or leaving this station will be considered an attack on Babylon 5 itself, and we will act accordingly.'

A transport leaves the station and passes by the Centauri vessel without being challenged. The staff in C and C break into a round of applause, but their relief is cut short as a Narn cruiser arrives through a jump point and powers up its weapons. Sheridan reaches for his console. 'We do not – repeat, do not – require assistance. Do not interfere.'

Maintenance 'bot cameras show the Narn cruiser fire at its Centauri counterpart. It turns and fires back. Shots exchange back and forth, lighting up C and C with explosions until the Centauri vessel is destroyed. The Narn cruiser tries to open a jump point, but it is hit badly. Ripples of energy from its jump engines surge along the ship, setting off a chain reaction of explosions that destroys the ship in a blaze of light.

Cynthia smiles into the camera at ISN Centre with some final thoughts on Babylon 5. 'There can be no question that it is a flashpoint that can only grow *hotter as time passes. And yet growth only comes through pain and struggle. So perhaps we should allow Babylon 5 time to realise, or one day, even exceed, the dreams we have invested in it,' she concludes. 'I'm Cynthia Torqueman, ISN News. Goodnight.'*

*B*abylon 5's usual method of storytelling is entirely put aside in 'And Now for a Word' as we get to see the space station as viewers of ISN would see it. It's a different view, an outsider's view, the view from Earth. 'It's a device that makes it more immediate by virtue of the news presentation,' says Joe Straczynski. 'It makes you feel like it's a media event. But because there are more closed doors and you don't see what's happening off-camera, you are more or less on the outside of the story to some extent. So it's a way of reversing the polarity of the feel of the whole show.'

It also served as an introductory episode for newer or more casual viewers. The newscast is packed with information about the station: its population, its layout, its function and its growing unpopularity. It recaps on a lot of background information, particularly with the Narn/Centauri conflict and the personal background of some of the characters.

Delenn is totally unprepared to face Earth's media. The harsh questions about her transformation reveal her vulnerability and uncertainty about the step she has taken. It was something Mira Furlan could relate to, having felt uncomfortable with the press back in former Yugoslavia. 'They're into sensation and they don't care about people, generally speaking. They don't want real answers. I never knew how to deal with them. I wanted to be like a good pupil, I wanted to say the truth, I really wanted to give a good in-depth answer and that's not what they're after. They're after something completely different and I didn't know. I just never had this talent of dealing with them. Maybe I was intimidated by them, but it showed as not being interested and being above the whole thing, being superior, and my superiority – which was actually my fear – was interpreted as rudeness, and then they were rude to me and I was rude to them and it went on. Then the war happened and I was this perfect target. In that way, I really could connect with that whole thing.'

In Londo, we see something different. This is not the Londo that we know: this is the public face of Londo, the politician who will defend his people and their actions to the hilt. 'That's an important element of Londo and what is wonderful is that it gets illustrated here,' says Peter Jurasik. 'For me, this was an easy show to play because I knew that I just lean on the public persona. It's just PR work for him. The easiest thing for Londo to do is to do PR and shout about the Centauri. He loves that. It is truly his ultimate passion, more than booze, more than women, more than anything else. His real passion is the Centauri.'

That contrasts very much with G'Kar, who also displays his public persona when he is in the council chamber or making a statement to the press, but when the reporter asks about his background, we get to see inside the person. It was a very moving scene and it was completed in just one take. 'Usually they ask you to come in and they do a rehearsal and then they light the set and come back and you have another couple of rehearsals,' explains Andreas Katsulus. 'I have to prepare all my words ahead of time because once I have the contact lenses in I can't see to read, so either I know them or I don't know them. So I had the speech totally memorized and the way I wanted to do it, and for some reason they were ready to shoot the scene. So they put me in the chair – no rehearsals or anything, which is a plus because a lot of your intention and what you've worked on gets dissipated with rehearsing it. It was just "sit down and do it" and I brought myself to the point of tears doing it. What was really funny was the wonderful actress who came in. She was supposed to be the hard-nosed object-ive reporter who doesn't get emotionally involved, and she was in tears!'

The reporter manages to get inside Dr Franklin, too, as he remembers his early days in space and his friend who accidentally spaced himself and died a horrific death. 'What I liked was that I was in Medlab and I was being asked something very emotional, very personal,' says Richard Biggs. 'I tried to get a sense of exhaustion, of being so tired that it just kind of seeps out. It's not some-thing that I really wanted to share, but I start talking about it because I'm so tired and so exhausted and so vulner-able that it starts to leak out.'

Sheridan, for the most part in his interview, was play-ing the statesman, putting forth the official line. But when asked if he thinks Babylon 5 is worth it, his reply is a per-sonal one about the need for humanity to be pioneering and look to the future. 'Joe gave me a marvellous speech,' remembers Bruce Boxleitner. 'It had to do with what I believe too ... Hopefully shows like this will inspire a different generation in another time to be spacefaring. We need to bring our eyes up off the horizon and to the stars again. That was kind of my philosophy and I knew it was his. We get bogged down in our problems here, we really do – all our nations, all our squabbles – and we must never forget that there is more exploration to do. Man's instinct is to always be going into the unknown to figure out what's out there and how it can help us.'

The episode is also memorable for Bruce for another reason. 'I had the worst day of my life on this show on that episode,' he says. 'I hadn't done TV series since 1987, which was the last series of *Scarecrow and Mrs King*, and I have now jammed so much dialogue through

my head with memorization that I was starting to freeze.
It would just go blank on me. There was this speech on
the Observation Dome where I was supposed to be con-
fronting an enemy-type ship – it was Centauri. There was
a speech that I had that was relatively no harder than anything else I've said in this show, but for some reason we
went twenty-seven takes. What happens with an actor is
I would get to this certain part – and now I know it's
coming – and it would fly away. It was like I was getting
Alzheimer's. And after about eight or nine takes, I get
very stubborn, I get very angry with myself, I have to get
very angry with myself to force myself. And so then
everybody just walked away. I had to go and take a walk
just to get away from it. It was horrible, absolutely horrible. I didn't want somebody to see this slate when
they're watching dailies that said "Take 27". There were
some camera problems with some of the takes. Then I
would get the whole speech and we'd have an airplane fly
over and it was no good for sound, or something like
that. It was jinxed.'

The episode pulled every trick of a news documentary,
from the straight interviews to pieces to camera (complete with people waving in the background), fly-on-the-
wall pieces and commentary from the studio. It then went
one better with the Psi Corps advert. Joe's idea was to
use it to indicate some of the subversive things happening on Earth. 'At first it was going to be an ordinary commercial. Then I thought, "Well let's make it the Psi Corps
and show how they are trying to present themselves."
And then on top of that I drop in a subliminal [message],
which is not, technically speaking, a subliminal. I had my
staff find out what constitutes subliminal material – and
it's two frames per second, which is illegal, you can't
do things at that speed – so I went four frames per
second ... A lot of good storytelling has to be, on some
level, subversive, and that definitely constitutes that.'

16:
'Knives'

Sheridan stoops down to look at a dead and bloody Markab in the part of the station that has come to be known as the 'Babylon triangle'. Without warning, the dead body reaches out and grabs Sheridan's face. He stumbles backwards, but not before a presence has passed between them.

Londo tenses as two arms grip him around the throat and hold him tight. 'Your doom, Paso,' says the figure behind him. A sense of recognition passes across Londo's face as he hears his old fighting name. 'Urza?' he says. The man bursts into laughter at his own practical joke and they embrace as two old friends.

Londo and Urza reminisce about old times over a drink or two. Then Urza explains why he has come to see Londo. He has been declared a traitor to the Centauri Republic and he needs Londo's support to save his family from disgrace.

Sheridan looks out from the Observation Dome as a ship appears in front of his eyes. It is the Icarus. *'Anna,' he whispers, recognizing his wife's ship. It explodes in a ball of orange light and Sheridan orders a scan of the area. The others look at him quizzically – they didn't see anything.*

The dead Markab had recently passed through the restricted sector of space where Babylon 4 disappeared. Sheridan reviews the station's visual record and freezes it on the image of Babylon 4 being pulled through time by a surge of white energy. A sudden rush of pain wells up in his mind and he turns to see his mother and father standing in his

quarters reaching out their arms to him. Then a surge
of white energy engulfs them and they are gone.

Sheridan gets in a Starfury and heads out towards
Sector 14, Babylon 4's last known position. He
encounters the time distortion and his cockpit begins
to shake. An opening appears ahead of him, ringed
by a glowing white line. Something causes Sheridan
to slam back against his pilot's seat. He cries out and
a white energy leaps out of his mouth – freezing him
in mid-scream – and streams towards the opening.
The alien life form that caused the illusions is gone.
It was just its way of saying it wanted to go home.

Londo joins Urza in a toast to the Centauri
Republic at a gathering to celebrate the alliance of
their two houses. But when Londo says the alliance
will not be necessary because he has spoken to Lord
Refa, Urza is disgusted. It is Refa who is
orchestrating his downfall. Nevertheless, Urza
presents Londo with a gift, a fine Centauri sword.
When Londo refuses to take it, Urza challenges him
to the 'Morago', a fight to the death.

Londo launches into an assault, and their swords
clash as each move is blocked by Urza. Urza fights
back, swiping his sword at Londo and cutting his
upper arm. He head-butts him and Londo falls to
the floor and looks up in terror to see Urza lifting
his sword ready for the kill. Instinctively, Londo
thrusts his blade into Urza's unprotected belly. He
collapses and Londo holds him in his arms. He has
won, and as tradition dictates, he must accept Urza's
family as his own. It means they will not be harmed
by Refa's scheming. 'I could not let them share my
disgrace,' Urza gasps. 'This way I die with honour
and you will see they are protected.' Londo watches
helplessly as his friend takes his last breath and dies
in his arms.

'Knives' is a breath of fresh air for Londo, with a glimpse of his old fun-loving self that was more typical of him in the first season. It begins with him and Vir enjoying themselves by singing a bit of Centauri opera. 'I cannot tell you how many times we had to practise that song,' says Peter Jurasik. 'I'll never forget that song. I could sing it for you right now, but I'd have to charge you a great deal of money!'

'They gave us the tune on a cassette and we had to learn it,' adds Stephen Furst, who plays Vir. 'We had to do the harmony and everything! We really put a good effort into that – it was like learning a foreign language. That was quite fun. I had such a good time doing that with him.'

The Centauri words were written in the script and the tune was composed by Christopher Franke, who does all of the scoring for *Babylon 5*. The style is very operatic because it takes its references from more down-to-Earth sources, as Peter Jurasik discovered. 'My father was visiting and he is an opera lover, so he was critical of how I was actually singing. He found some riffs within the music that reminded him of some opera and he eventually made a tape of some of the songs and sent it to me and I could hear what he was talking about.'

There is more revelry when Londo's old friend arrives and they take the chance to sit down and reminisce about their youth over a drink or two. Peter remembers working to develop a believable on-screen relationship with Carmen Argenziano who played Urza Jaddo. 'An aspect to all of this work on every episode – but this was a particularly good one to note because we were playing particularly good friends – is trying to establish relationships with guest actors when they arrive on the set. You're supposed to know them, or like them, or hate them – or feel anything for them! They just arrive on the set and you have to work, and that was a really good example of how hard Carmen and I worked to put a sense of relationship to it.'

The idea of bringing an old friend of Londo's aboard the station came from the writer, Lawrence G. DiTillio, who sensed he was becoming an unsympathetic character. 'When we had seen the Centauri we had seen them as villains,' says Larry. 'Except for Vir, every Centauri was the same arrogant snot who hated the Narns and I thought, "Wouldn't it be interesting if some guy comes who is an old friend of Londo's, who is on the other side, who doesn't want to blast the Narns? Who really wants to get along with them, who detests the infighting that's going on with the Centauri rule, who doesn't realize Londo is the linchpin?" But Londo knows it and he's torn when this guy comes and asks for help.'

It makes Londo reflect on the type of person he has become by remembering the type of person he used to be. He also comes to realize the sort of people he has allied himself to when he discovers that it is Refa who is selling out his old friend in the name of gaining power.

It leads to a fight to the death between the two old friends, meaning that the two actors had to take up swords and stage a fight in the middle of the studio. 'Not only were we supposed to be able to fight with them, but Carmen and I were supposed to be expert at it!' says Peter. 'That's always a lovely thing for them to impose on a character: "Now I have to be *expert* at this too?" So it takes a fair amount of practice and you really have to throw yourself into it, but be careful. We had a ball doing it, it was a lot of fun. It's another aspect of being an actor. Instead of going through our pedestrian routine lives, I'm standing with another guy with this sword and we're fighting to the death.'

When Londo is forced to kill Urza, he is faced with one of the personal consequences of Refa's scheming. He has lost another friend to his new-found ambition. 'I think it was a good showcase for Centauri society and for Londo's growing isolation,' comments J. Michael Straczynski. 'Power tends to cost one one's friends. It was a good sympathetic episode for him. We got to show him being physical, which we didn't often do with Londo. The "B" story wasn't quite as successful.'

The 'B' story, or subplot, was Sheridan's being possessed by an alien. 'Originally I wanted to do a thing where Sheridan's father has a serious illness,' says Larry DiTillio, 'but Joe figured we were knocking off too many family members at that time and he suggested that Sheridan be possessed by an alien force. I wasn't quite as enthused with it, but I went with it the best that I could. And when I came out with that gaseous creature, and Joe added the thing about coming out of the rift around Babylon 4, it got a little more interesting for me. I wanted Sheridan to make first contact with a race without realizing he was making first contact with a race. And I had planned to bring those gaseous creatures back and show that they appreciated what Sheridan did for them, but I never stayed on the show.'

The creature taps into Sheridan's mind for images of fear, loss and home to try to convey a message to its human host. Many of the things he sees – blurred images, the explosion of his wife's ship and the Grylor that attacks him – were created after the fact by CGI. It is relatively easy to understand how an actor might react to something he is supposed to be seeing through the Observation Dome window, but how do you fight an alien bird that isn't there? 'In your imagination,' says Bruce Boxleitner. 'I had to create it in my mind, what it might be. We had a general description of it, a pterodactyl-type thing – and "here it comes, it's swooping down" and the director would go "it's coming" and I would duck and roll around on the cement floor.'

There was more imagination involved for Sheridan's

baseball session. Not only was the baseball field CGI, but the balls were too. 'I intentionally used a very heavy bat so I'd get a workout doing it,' says Bruce. 'Whereas Jerry walked up with the lightest bat in the whole group! Of course, I hit more fair balls than he did; they put in a lot of foul balls that he hit. I love baseball.'

Bruce's love of baseball was the inspiration for those scenes. At the beginning, the writers had sat down with the actors and talked about their background with a view to using some of that in the series. Jerry Doyle's love of cooking transferred to Garibaldi, Richard Biggs's father was the inspiration for bringing Franklin's father on board in 'GROPOS' and Larry DiTillio wanted to play to Bruce's strengths in 'Knives' by giving him a chance to play baseball. 'Blues Chicago Cubs is [the shirt] he is wearing and that's what he's a fan of,' says Larry. 'Originally, I had intended that scene not to be a full baseball field, which I thought was silly for a space station where space is at a premium, but John Copeland [the producer] wanted to do a full ball field. I was going to do a batting cage that had strange holographic balls come out of it and you hit them into planets and stuff, but they didn't want to do it that way.'

It extended Sheridan's character a little by showing him off duty and game to investigate a mystery, even though Garibaldi thinks he shouldn't. It reminds the audience of the Babylon 4 mystery, which was largely put on the back burner in the second season, but was to return in the third. It also reacquaints us with what happened to Anna Sheridan and the *Icarus* in preparation for Sheridan's encounter with a living member of the *Icarus*'s crew – Morden – in 'In the Shadow of Z'ha'dum'.

17:
'In the Shadow of Z'ha'dum'

*Garibaldi interrupts Sheridan as he is sorting
through some of his wife's effects left behind after
she died on the* Icarus. *Garibaldi takes a look at the
ship's inventory and recognizes the face of one of
the crew who supposedly died. It is Morden.*

*Morden is sitting calmly in the interrogation room
with Sheridan sitting opposite him. Sheridan pushes
a photograph of his wife across the table and then
taps his link, bringing up a news report on the
monitor of the destruction of the* Icarus. *Morden
admits he was part of the crew, but somehow
survived and was found floating unconscious in an
EVA suit next to the wreckage. Sheridan doesn't
believe him. 'One hundred and thirty-nine people
died on board the* Icarus, *Mr Morden, including my
wife. And here you sit, not a scratch. Something here
doesn't add up. I intend to find out what happened,
what* really *happened.'*

*Pierce Macabee has arrived from Earth's newly
created Ministry of Peace to preach their Night
Watch concept to the station. People who wear the
armband will be Earth's eyes and ears, looking out
for anything that might threaten peace. By the end
of his speech he has converted a significant portion
of station personnel. 'Fifty extra credits for walking
around and doing what I do anyway?' shrugs a
security guard, Zack Allen. 'Why not?'*

*Delenn and Kosh demand that Morden be
released. But Sheridan has gone too far to turn back*

*without some answers, and Delenn realizes it has
come time to explain.*

*Delenn tells him about a war a thousand years
ago in which the Minbari ancient races, known as
the First Ones, and others united to defeat a race
known as the Shadows. They are now preparing for
another war, slowly building their forces at
Z'ha'dum.*

*Kosh turns to Sheridan and projects an energy
beam into his mind. He sees the* Icarus *and the crew
on a planet's surface surrounded by stone ruins.
They investigate an opening in the surface and inside
the darkness something stirs. It raises its deep-black,
almost reptilian head and its eyes widen with a soft
glow. Kosh releases the energy beam and Sheridan
stumbles backwards as the image fades from his
mind.*

*'Once awakened, the Shadows could not allow
them to leave,' Delenn explains. 'Those who would
not serve were killed.' Morden is now their servant
and he must be released before the Shadows realize
how much they know. 'Aside from the Vorlons, we
don't have the First Ones to help us this time. We
are on our own. We will only have one chance to
stop them, and we must be ready.'*

*Sheridan stares at Morden's image on the monitor
from where security cameras look down on him in
the cell. He thinks about what Delenn said and gets
Zack to scan the room on different frequencies.
Static distorts the picture before clearing and
revealing something else in the room – two, deep-
black, spindly creatures. Sheridan leaps up and
stares at them as their images fade from the screen.*

*Sheridan lets Morden go and tells Kosh what he
has done. 'But there's a price tag attached,' he says.
'I want you to teach me how to fight them. How to*

> *beat them. Because sooner or later I'm going to*
> *Z'ha'dum, and I'm going to stop them.'*
>
> *'If you go to Z'ha'dum, you will die,' Kosh*
> *replies. But Sheridan is resolute and the Vorlon*
> *agrees to teach him.*

The death of Sheridan's wife which, it had seemed, was just there to give Sheridan's character a little depth when it was planted back in the second episode, takes on a greater significance in 'In the Shadow of Z'ha'dum'. To find that Morden was also on the ship and survived throws a different light on the fate of the *Icarus*. If Morden survived, could Anna Sheridan have survived too? And if Morden was turned into a servant of the Shadows, what really happened to the *Icarus*?

When Sheridan finds out about Morden, his world is turned upside down and he is prepared to do anything, to the point of abusing his position, to find out the truth. 'This is the episode when we knocked the smile off Sheridan,' says Joe Straczynski. 'When we first brought him on he was all chipper and happy and just glad to be there, and over the season there was a process ongoing of removing that smirk from his face ... I wanted to show-case that this is not your average commander or officer who would do what was right and by the rules. He was willing to sacrifice everything to find out the facts here. It was only when Delenn made it clear to him that the stakes were higher than he imagined, higher than his career, higher than his job, that he turned around.'

'I like that about him,' says the actor Bruce Boxleitner. 'He isn't such a goody-goody guy. In television you walk a fine line: I'm playing the hero and the hero does have certain limitations. The bad people, or "the bad guys" or whatever you want to call them, can tend to be a little more colourful. You only have certain colours that you can play and if you step over that line then you're not a good guy and people think, "I really don't like this guy and I've been pulling for him all along." I, myself, would prefer a little more of that.'

The interrogation scenes between Sheridan and Morden are an escalating display of emotion with Sheridan getting increasingly heated as Morden continues to rebuff his questions with a calm assuredness. Perhaps it is because Morden knows that, legally, Sheridan can't touch him, and maybe it is because he feels safe surrounded by his unseen Shadow masters. 'It never really feels like there's a lot at stake for Morden,' says the actor Ed Wasser. 'He's so cool, so collected, so in control. The scene with Bruce gets a little hot. There's a little mind game going on between Bruce and I, and it's the first time there's any confrontation, the first time that Morden gets some meat to play with.'

It was also the first episode directed by David Eagle, who was later to become a regular visitor to *Babylon 5*. He hadn't directed any science fiction before, but had been a fan since he was a teenager, reading extensively and making an effort to see every SF film and TV show he possibly could. 'Doing that show was a lot of fun for me,' he says. 'It was a dream come true, to do science fiction and to get my feet wet doing that particular show ... I remember Joe saying to me, "David, this is a pivotal episode" and feeling the pressure.'

David Eagle watched around thirty episodes to get to know *Babylon 5* intimately and used them as a reference when he came to formulate his approach to the interrogation scenes. 'I wanted that intensity and I think they had done one or two interrogation scenes prior to that particular one and I looked at those and the way they were lit, the way the camera moved and so on. I wanted to emulate what I saw and bring something new to it at the same time. Also, this was Bruce's first season as the commander of *Babylon 5* and he was feeling his oats as that character and I think in that episode his strengths really come out. In that interrogation in particular I think he just did an absolutely wonderful job.'

Sheridan takes the whole matter further than anyone is prepared to follow him. His staff are loyal to him, but their loyalty – at this stage at least – doesn't go beyond their duty to Earthforce. Garibaldi temporarily resigns because he cannot stand by while the rules about holding prisoners are openly violated, and Ivanova warns him that she will report him if his behaviour continues. He is so single-minded on the issue, however, and so affected by the death of his wife, that he is prepared to sacrifice everything for the truth.

When Talia Winters refuses to telepathically scan Morden, Sheridan arranges for her to pass him in the corridor where she senses the Shadows. 'That scene I shot somewhat differently from the way it ended up,' says David Eagle. 'I shot that scene when she sees the Shadows and screams and faints from about five or six different angles. My idea was to make that moment when she screams much bigger than it was, to do an over-exaggeration where you see the same moment three or four times from the different angles and they're quickly flashed right in front of you. It expands that moment rather than contracting it. That's the way I shot it and that's the way I cut it in my director's cut, but for various reasons – I think both time and creative reasons – it was cut back by the producers.'

Talia's reaction to being used in that way was to slap Sheridan around the face. It was not something the actress Andrea Thompson enjoyed doing. 'No, because he's such a sweet guy,' she says. 'I'm a very strong person and sometimes I'm not aware of my strength, and although I felt like I wasn't hitting him very hard, I was probably hitting him harder than he expected me to hit. It's a fine line: you don't want it to look fake, but at the same time you don't want to hurt your fellow actors.'

'I did a show on Broadway where I had to have that happen every night,' says Bruce Boxleitner. 'The real trick is not to anticipate it. You have to be surprised every time. Well, that's not natural to anybody once you know something's coming. You have to put your chin out there and let her do it. She knocked me out cold once. The first take she hit me so hard – she backed off a little on the second one – but the first take she hit me and then there was supposed to be a long silence and I was supposed to say a line. My brain was rattling around, thinking "What is the line? What is the line?"'

'Then they wanted to shoot it one more time,' remembers Andrea, 'and Bruce went, "No, I don't think so, I think you have this one." I felt so bad afterwards, I went around the rest of the day apologizing to him.'

Sheridan's resolve is only halted when Delenn and Kosh tell him why he must release Morden. It is a pivotal moment because the Shadow threat had been building for a season and a half. There had been glimpses of mysterious ships in hyperspace, attacks against the Narns, the power of Morden's 'associates', all hinting that something was going on, but without a context they meant very little. Here is confirmation of the alien threat that G'Kar had been talking about, and the truth about Z'ha'dum.

In providing these answers, the episode pointed to the next phase of the story, getting prepared for the Shadow war. It also, less obviously, foreshadows other events. Delenn mentions that Kosh, as one of the First Ones, cannot leave his encounter suit because he will be recognized, and this anticipates his eventual appearance in 'The Fall of Night'. And with the true nature of events surrounding the *Icarus* revealed, it hinted at the possibility that Anna Sheridan could return. '[The playwright] Anton Chekhov had the rule that if you shoot a gun in Act

Three, Scene One, you must show the gun on the wall in Act One, Scene Two,' says Joe Straczynski, 'and this was putting the gun on the wall so I could fire it off later on.'

18:
'Confessions and Lamentations'

Four Markabs have died from apparent 'natural causes' over the past three days and Dr Franklin is suspicious. When an in-depth autopsy confirms his suspicions, he marches on the Markab's doctor and demands to know the truth. 'The disease is one hundred per cent terminal,' says Dr Lazarenn soberly, 'and one hundred per cent contagious.'

The disease has struck only once before, on an isolated island, and wiped itself out when the islanders died. Over time it became a legend and it was believed that only the immoral would be touched by it. When new cases emerged, families were too scandalized to report it and too convinced of their own morality to be concerned. Lazarenn and others have been working on a cure without support from their government. 'They don't even want to talk about it,' he tells Franklin, 'as though the very subject makes them dirty.'

Nobody knows if the disease will attack other species. If it is airborne, the station's recycled air means the whole place could be infected and if they segregate the Markab population from everyone else, it will only help the disease to spread among the Markab.

Franklin begins a full-scale examination of every Markab on the station, much to the anger of the Markab ambassador. He feels Franklin is implying that they are immoral and decides to shut all of his people away in an isolation zone where they can be *away from the immorality of other races.*

Delenn visits Sheridan in his quarters with a request that makes him go cold. She wants to enter the isolation zone to do all she can to help. Sheridan knows she will be exposing herself to mass contamination and he lowers his eyes. 'Do not look away, Captain,' she says. 'If I do not see you again here, I will see you in a little while, in the place where no shadows fall.' She turns and, before she leaves, they share a look which they both know may be their last.

The fear is written on the faces of Franklin's staff as they hesitate to enter the isolab where a Pak'ma'ra lies dead, a possible victim of the disease. Franklin is ready to go in himself until Lazarenn walks through the door and volunteers. He has not been in there long before a dizziness overcomes him and he realizes that he is infected.

The tests on the Pak'ma'ra reveal what they had all feared – the disease has jumped species. To Franklin, this is more information to help him fight this thing, and he gets the computer to run through every possible comparison between the two species. Meanwhile, Lazarenn gets weaker. 'Yellow cells,' he murmurs and Franklin approaches him with a glimmer of hope. But the Markab doctor is too far gone. 'I'm sorry, old friend. I don't think I can stay any longer. Give my love to —' And he is gone.

Franklin turns away in exasperation and lashes out at the nearest thing – a trolley of medical equipment – which crashes to the floor. At this point of desperation, the computer's voice chimes in: it has found a connection between the Markabs and the Pak'ma'ra.

Franklin develops a drug which will enable susceptible species to withstand the disease and *hurries down to the isolation zone with Sheridan and Ivanova. They step inside and are met by a horrific sight – all the Markabs are dead.*

Delenn and Lennier stagger out from among the bodies. Delenn looks up into Sheridan's face. 'John …' is all she can manage before the emotion overwhelms her and she cries on his shoulder.

'Oh God, what a nightmare that one was!' exclaims Bill Mumy, who plays Lennier. 'It was hot. We had, like, ninety extras working. I'm not trying to be gross about this – but it's true – those Markabs didn't have mouths! Anyway, somebody threw up in their mask. It's true, it's absolutely true, and people were passing out from the heat. Mira and I, we literally felt like Gandhi amongst a bunch of lepers because these people were really, truly, honestly suffering. It was a gross physical set. It just stank.'

Kevin G. Cremin, who was production manager for the second season, was also the director on this episode and was really keen to get as many Markabs crammed in there as possible. 'I went to John [Vulich, who deals with prosthetics] and said, "I know you've been doing really well in your department. How many Markabs can you give me?" Obviously we wanted to see as many as you could pack into the screen – it just got more effective the more you could see. So he said, "How many do you want?" I remember looking at him and saying, "Can you do fifty?" I remember everyone at the table – Ann in costumes nearly fell off her chair! – and everybody was, "Oh God, no, we have other shows to do." But they kind of gave me a wink and said, "Kev, for you, we'll make fifty." I remember hearing the guys were working around the clock just casting Markab heads as quickly as possible. They just went the extra yard for me and I very much appreciated that.'

With a disease spreading wildly through the Markab population, the onus was very much on Dr Franklin to come up with an answer. 'That's Joe going, "OK, let's see if he can handle forty pages of scientific dialogue!"' laughs Richard Biggs. 'All those six-syllable words – that was a challenge.'

'I like the ending,' he adds. 'I know a lot of people were going to say, "Ah, Franklin is going to come through and the cavalry's going to be there and they're going to get the cure and everything's going to be peachy" and I liked the fact that we had the answer, but we had the answer just a little late. I like surprising the audience. I think that's the best thing about *Babylon 5*: the answer's not always going to be there and, even if we have the answer, it may just be a little late. The ending is not going to be what you think it is. I love that because I grew up on TV and there's a structure to TV that you get bored with. After the first ten minutes of an hour show you're, like, "I know exactly what's going to happen" and sure enough you're way ahead of them and you're, like, "Yeah great" as you fall asleep before the ending. *Babylon 5* is a little different. Joe is saying "This is the way it is", the kid dies, the whole race of people die. Things like this happen in real life and we're not afraid to show it.'

The sheer scale of the devastation is shown when Franklin and the cavalry enter the Markab isolation zone to see a huge room full of dead bodies. Although we later hear that the whole race has been wiped out, it is merely a coda to this image. What gives it extra impact is that, over the course of the episode, we got to know two individual Markabs who succumb to the disease. Dr Lazarenn, after initially keeping the truth from Franklin, makes the supreme sacrifice by carrying out an autopsy on a diseased body, making his death more poignant. There was also the little girl who contracted the disease, proving that germs don't care who they infect.

It was a rare thing to have a child on *Babylon 5*, particularly an alien child. It hadn't been done since 'Believers', partly because of the logistical problems of using children on a film set. 'You only have a minor for so many hours in the day,' explains Kevin Cremin. 'If so many of those hours are spent in the make-up chair – and she spent two hours in the make-up chair – that cuts her effective work day down to two hours a day. The scheduling problems on that one were great. I remember John [Radulovic] was the assistant director and we were drilling him the week before production. We went through his production board with a fine-tooth comb trying to make sure that we could get her days worked out to where they were doable, where we could get her on camera and still get the full make-up on her and she was wonderful.'

Most of the child's scenes are with Delenn, who showed the side of herself that Mira Furlan enjoys most. 'That's one of my favourites,' she says, 'the warm Delenn. I liked the whole relationship with the little child. There was a lot of sadness and a lot of good points. A great metaphor for our society dealing with AIDS, for example, even with cancer, with illness as such. Our society is afraid of it in general. Sick people are isolated. I know about illnesses through my mother, who was ill and so on. And the relationship between Sheridan and her, there was a beautiful little scene about meeting afterwards in another life.'

The experience brings out Delenn's and Sheridan's true feelings for each other. When Delenn tells Sheridan she is going to lock herself in with the dying Markabs, the concern he shows is more than a captain's concern for an ambassador. Later, when she emerges from among the Markab bodies and cries on his shoulder, they are closer than they have ever been before.

That development is an important one in terms of the

story arc and is demonstrated within the episode in the contrast between their relationship at the end and the uneasiness with which they share a Minbari meal. The scene became something of an in joke that they kept talking about long after the episode was finished. Bruce Boxleitner remembers that, for some reason, he and Bill Mumy found something funny about the Minbari food, 'flarn'. 'That's where Billy and I spent most of the time while we were lighting that scene, substituting the word 'love' for 'flarn' in every Beatles song we could sing: "Can't buy me flarn ..." Anyway, we made the entire crew sick! They wanted us to get the hell out of there, but we had to do the scene.'

Sheridan was taken away from the meal by another station emergency and afterwards Delenn and Lennier exchanged some puzzled Minbari words which weren't in the script. 'We had this little comment, Billy and I, which we wanted to do in Minbari,' remembers Mira. 'We thought, "Let's speak Minbari. Why are we always speaking English when we are alone?" I guess the characters don't speak in their own native tongues because Americans don't want to read subtitles.'

The episode became one of the most successful of the season, and certainly generated a great deal of debate among viewers. Many took it to be a comment on the AIDS virus, but this is just a more recent example of the way humanity deals with disease. 'The point of reference in the episode, in fact, is the black plague,' says Joe Straczynski. 'We have a nasty tendency to attack the victim instead of the disease, and whatever the context of the black plague, AIDS, Ebola, whatever it happens to be, the moment you politicize the germ, you've lost the battle. You have to set all that aside. And this takes that stupid tendency to attach morality to that which is outside the moral sphere to its ultimate extreme. They created for themselves a situation where they couldn't admit the problem because to admit the problem would admit more failings on their part. I think that's an important lesson to get across, whatever disease we're talking about. I made a point to wipe out the entire species except for a couple on a distant colony somewhere. I said we should have a mass burial for all the Markab prosthetics and costumes – it wasn't received too well!'

19:
'Divided Loyalties'

It has taken two years for Ivanova and Talia to become friends, but now they have put their hostilities aside and are sharing breakfast at the Eclipse Café. 'All you had to do was admit that you were wrong and I was right and everything would have been fine!' Ivanova says with a smile. Talia smiles back, but she is interrupted by Ivanova's link. Duty calls.

A ship has entered the jumpgate and made no attempt to contact the station. It is pulled in and they find one person unconscious, but alive, on board. It is Lyta Alexander, Babylon 5's former commercial telepath.

Lyta wakes up as Franklin treats her and jumps off the medbed, backing away from him. 'I want to see Captain Sheridan now,' she screams, grabbing a syringe to protect herself from him. 'Someone here – one of you – is a traitor.'

Lyta had been recalled to Earth by the Psi Corps two years ago after she scanned Ambassador Kosh following the attempt on his life. She managed to escape and find her way to Mars. There, she got involved with the revolutionary movement and found out about the Psi Corps's sleeper programme. It creates a false personality strong enough to hide a spy's true identity, even from themselves. Lyta has reason to believe one of these agents has been planted on Babylon 5, and she has the telepathic password that can prove it.

Sheridan returns to his quarters at the end of a long day and is halfway across the room when he *notices Ivanova sitting on his sofa. She has let herself in. She begins to say something, but the words will not come. Then, slowly and painfully, she tells him what she has hidden since she was a child. 'I can't have Lyta or any other telepath in my mind. Ever. I'm a latent telepath.'*

Ivanova stands to avoid Sheridan's gaze, feeling the weight of what she has told him. 'I'm probably not even a P1,' she says. 'I can block a casual scan and I know instantly if someone is doing it, nothing more. But it's enough for the Psi Corps to pull you in.' Sheridan stands to console her. Then he remembers his dream of Ivanova asking, 'Do you know who I am?' Was this what Kosh was trying to tell him?

Sheridan agrees for Lyta to check Babylon 5's command staff for the false personality. She sends the password into the minds of all of them – Sheridan, Franklin, Garibaldi – but achieves nothing. Ivanova stands there as all the subsidiary staff come in and out of the office and are probed to no effect. Lyta says that as they move away from the centre of power, the chances of finding the spy become less likely and, inevitably, she turns to Ivanova. Ivanova sighs deeply and braces herself. 'I'll do it,' she says. Lyta pushes hard to get the telepathic signal through Ivanova's instinctive blocks, and pulls out with a jolt. 'She's clean,' says Lyta. 'I'm sorry ...'

Talia walks in in search of the captain and Lyta locks eyes with her. Before Talia can shield herself, she sends the password. Talia's hands go to her temples as pain runs through her mind. 'Oh my God, it's her!' says Lyta as Garibaldi grabs Talia and drags her out.

Ivanova visits Talia, but all she finds is a callous

personality, glad to emerge from out of the shadows of the person she calls her 'invisible sister'. 'You're right,' says Ivanova, hurt and betrayed. 'The Talia I knew is dead.'

The dramatic departure of Talia Winters from *Babylon 5* was something forced on the production when the actress Andrea Thompson decided to leave. 'It was very tough for me,' she admits. 'I was willing to hang out for two years and be a very small part of the story. I'd go in to work maybe once every couple of months and spend the rest of the time with my son. But my son had gone off to school and I found myself sitting home alone – and I like to work. So I talked to them about it and there was just no way that Talia was going to be around more than she had been ... I was seeing new characters being introduced and guest stars would have more going on than I did and I said, "I can't stay."'

It meant having to write Talia out of the show, something which Joe Straczynski shrugs off as one of the realities of making television. 'I have included life as a random factor in the show,' he explains. 'When things like this happen, when the actor feels she isn't getting enough lines and wants to go – and you don't want to have an unhappy actress on the show – I tend to embrace it. I feel it's OK, this is a challenge for the show ... That randomness, I think, works for us sometimes because it leaves viewers never quite sure where it's going to go and who's going to make it through to the end of the story. I figure if *Babylon 5* were a real story, these things might happen. Sheridan might get hit by a truck – it happens! Why not take advantage of that?'

Advantage was duly taken and Talia was given one of the best episodes of the season to go out on. Talia was a member of an organization that many people find horrific, but over the course of two years, the audience got to know her as a person and saw her as separate from the Psi Corps to some degree. That is nowhere more evident than in 'A Race Through Dark Places', where she joins with a group of rogue telepaths to dupe the psi cop, Bester. Her friendship with Ivanova is getting closer and Sheridan is ready to invite her to join their cell group, when it is all undermined by the revelation of Talia's true personality. It maximizes the dramatic impact and, although it comes in time to save the command staff from exposure to a Psi Corps spy, Ivanova is not saved from the feelings of hurt and betrayal.

The relationship between Ivanova and Talia had progressed from open hostility on Ivanova's part to an easy friendship. They are so close by 'Divided Loyalties' that Ivanova invites Talia to stay in her quarters when her own are out of order. There was little indication up to this point that their relationship had progressed this far, and was a jump that, in an ideal world, would have happened more gradually. 'I would have liked to have [seen] that relationship a little more and built it a little more,' says Joe. 'I was building it very gradually over two years because I wanted to realistically build a context where you could go from mutual dislike to being involved with each other. I had to pull that trigger about nine episodes before I would have preferred to.'

The clear implication is that the liaison went further than just friendship. Although some viewers thought Talia merely slept over, the scene where she wakes up and puts her hand across to the opposite pillow to find Ivanova gone, reveals that it was more than that. Lesbianism is still a bit of a taboo subject on American TV, but that didn't bother Claudia Christian. 'I didn't have a problem with it at all – I mean, Andrea's a babe!' says the actress. 'I wanted for children to be able to watch it and not pick it up, but I wanted adults to be able to watch it and make up their own minds. I thought it was realistically and sensitively portrayed. I've grown up in gay communities my entire life. I went to high school in Laguna Beach and I live in West Hollywood now. It's not exactly something that is surprising or shocking to me, nor is it even something that I think about. Either you're a couple or you're not. I'm very open-minded. Andrea and I had fun during takes, we'd screw around, get the men all hot and bothered. And then she went and married Jerry! So I lost my woman – to Garibaldi no less!'

Andrea Thompson, who did indeed go on to marry her fellow *Babylon 5* cast member Jerry Doyle, thought the episode could have gone even further. 'I had no problem when they told me my character was gay or bisexual, but if we're going to do it, don't do it just for ratings, do it because you want to bring some bit of truth or reality to this. A relationship is a relationship and I don't care if it's between two men, two women, or a man and a woman. Love is love. But I felt a little duped because I said she should kiss the girl, because if this was a guy you'd have me sucking face with this guy. I said, "If you're going to do it, let us do the kiss", but they wouldn't do it.'

'I didn't want to exploit it, or make it something for titillation – it was just something that happened,' explains Joe Straczynski. 'Some people got very upset afterward and said, "You have a strong female character in Ivanova. How come she has to be gay to pull this off?" She's not, she's flexible, and a lot of people have momentary liaisons with their own sex. That doesn't necessarily make them gay.'

The episode also saw the return of *Babylon 5*'s original telepath Lyta Alexander. Since appearing in the pilot, the actress Patricia Tallman had had a baby and worked doing stunts and appearing on the stage, and she was excited about coming back. She was also very nervous. 'My first day on the set, I haven't been in front of the camera and done this in two years. I have four pages of dialogue and it's huge speeches,' she says. 'There was a lot of technical stuff that I had to make real somehow and then Bruce would have one line like, "And then what happened?" And then I'd talk again for another twenty minutes and then Claudia would go "uh ha" and then I'd talk again and Richard actually fell asleep on the couch! We were shooting it all morning, too. It was a big huge scene and I had to say this over and over and over again. They were just so wonderful, they were so supportive, they would laugh and make jokes.'

Lyta developed a trademark telepathic stare on 'Divided Loyalties', which she used when she was probing somebody's mind. The whole thing came about by accident and she gets teased about it to this day. 'I don't want to give that away, but mostly what that is is that I'm extremely near-sighted. The director was saying, "I can't tell when you're reading somebody else's mind. I think you need to focus more," and when I went [squint] to look at them he said "Good!" I didn't know what I did! Then I finally realized what I was doing and I was laughing because I'm basically looking at people a little more. Then it became a big joke. Bruce was making fun of me. We had that big scene where we're looking at each other and he'd call someone in and they'd look at each other and I'd go [squint] and Bruce was going [squint].'

The return of Lyta was an unexpected turn that was able to draw on all the things that had been laid down during her first appearance, particularly regarding her relationship with Kosh. It pointed to further appearances and a possible replacement for Talia as a telepathic presence on *Babylon 5*. Ivanova's dramatic revelation of her own telepathic abilities suggested more possibilities. Once again Joe Straczynski closed one door in his story arc just to open two others.

20:
'The Long, Twilight Struggle'

The war is faring even worse for the Narn than they will admit to their own people. In an attempt to fight back, they plan to draw off forces from the defence of the Narn homeworld to strike on the Centauri's supply stronghold, Gorash 7.

Lord Refa's sources on Centauri Prime have found out what the Narn plan to do and he sees the ideal opportunity to strike at their homeworld. All he needs Londo to do is ensure his 'allies' are waiting for the Narns at Gorash 7. Londo is hesitant – his 'allies' have begun to worry him – but Refa will hear none of it. 'Now is not the time for doubts, Mollari,' he says. 'We are here because of you. It's a little late to back out now.'

One of the Narn refugees passing through Babylon 5 tells Dr Franklin he was interrogated by the Centauri about the defences of the Narn homeworld before the Centauri inexplicably withdrew from the Dross colony. G'Kar knows this is not the Centauri's usual strategy and fears the worst, but his appeals to stop the attack on Gorash 7 and protect the Narns go unheeded.

All G'Kar can do is pray. When the Narn fleet arrives at the Gorash system, they are met by five Shadow vessels that shimmer into view ahead of them. G'Kar sits at his desk with the Book of G'Quan open before him as a Shadow vessel launches dozens of fighters that advance like deadly black specks. G'Kar murmurs a prayer urgently, his *lips moving faster and faster, as the Narn ships are destroyed in a barrage of fire. The last two Narn cruisers try to escape into hyperspace, but the Shadow vessels fire energy weapons into the heart of the jump points and the cruisers are crushed in their collapse. Back in his room, G'Kar opens his eyes and looks down at his holy book. His prayer is finished.*

The Centauri fleet fly towards the Narn homeworld, powering up their mass drivers and shooting their cargo towards the planet below. Each ball of destruction glows hot as it passes through the atmosphere and crashes onto the surface. Londo watches all this from the bridge of the Centauri victory ship, his face heavy with the weight of what he has done.

Londo returns to Babylon 5, standing tall in victory, while G'Kar sits in the Council Chamber with his head bowed. The Narn regime has surrendered. Londo lays down terms, to disband the ruling Kha'ri and put its members on trial; execute five hundred Narns if any Narn murders a Centauri; and set up their own ruling council on the Narn homeworld. Finally, he demands that G'Kar be stripped of his ambassadorial title and be sent back to Narn for trial.

On that final matter, Sheridan refuses. G'Kar has asked for sanctuary and is protected by the neutrality of Babylon 5. Nevertheless, Londo demands that G'Kar leave the chamber without delay. G'Kar raises his head and stands. 'No dictator, no invader, can hold an imprisoned population by force of arms for ever,' he says. 'Though it take a thousand years, we will be free.' With that, he walks out proudly.

Sheridan enters the Conference Centre to find

himself surrounded by human and Minbari Rangers.
They are, Delenn tells him, the first line of defence
in the war that is to come. She offers Sheridan equal
command, which he accepts. 'A line has been drawn
against the darkness,' he tells the crowd, 'and we
will hold that line no matter the cost.'

The title for this episode comes from a speech made by the former US president John F. Kennedy. 'It was very much emblematic,' says Joe Straczynski. 'If you wipe the original Kennedy quote, it sort of hints at the direction of the show.'

That quote is: 'Now the trumpet summons us again. Not as a call to bear arms, though arms we need. Not as a call to battle, though in battle we are. But as a call to bear the burdens of a long, twilight struggle, year in and year out, rejoicing in hope, patient in tribulation, a struggle against the common enemies of man: tyranny, poverty, disease and war itself.'

The title also takes the story further into darkness. We are at the twilight moment before night falls. The Centauri attack has taken the galaxy further along that path, but there is still a hint of daylight. War is still contained between the two races. But, as Londo sits and listens to the ISN report of Centauri plans to seize several smaller worlds on the border of Narn space, it is clear that the war may not be isolated for long and that daylight may soon be just a memory.

It is a dark moment for Londo. He has come to understand the deadly force that his 'allies', the Shadows, represent, but he isn't quite ready to make a stand and reject that power. There is an inner conflict going on for Londo between the politician who wants to see the Centauri race rule the galaxy and the person who senses the dark path he is treading. Never is that more powerfully shown than here. Refa invites Londo to watch the destruction of Narn from the head of the fleet. The politician inside Londo cannot refuse the invitation, but as he stands alone looking out of the window, the feelings of the person inside are written across his face.

'I love to talk about that because it was a brilliant piece of directing by John Flinn,' says Peter Jurasik, who plays Londo. 'Here I was, having learned my lessons from "Soul Mates" of pushing too much [in order to please the director], I thought, "I'm not going to push." But what he did was he put me on a ten-foot-tall platform and just left me up there. Talk about isolation for the character! He just left me up on the platform and gave me plenty of time to stare out and think of the backstory and what was underlying it. So if that scene works at all – and we've got enough response that I guess it does – the tributes go to John Flinn.'

What gives the scene added impact is the reflections on the window. As we look at Londo's face through the window we also see reflections of the Centauri battle cruisers outside. And as we look over Londo's shoulder to the scene below, we see his expression reflected in the glass. It was both dramatically effective and technically impressive to combine these two images in the same frame. 'I really wanted to get his reflections,' says John Flinn. 'I said, "Put up a piece of plexiglass and I want to photograph that into the blue screen." Then it hit me about half an hour before doing the scene. I thought, "Oh God, this is going to be hard. This is really going to be hard." And it just came off.'

The episode marks a turn in the Narn/Centauri conflict as the Narn surrender to the Centauri. It is the final reversal of the impression given in the very first episode, 'Midnight on the Firing Line', where it seemed the Narn were the aggressor and the Centauri the victims. Now the Centauri have hit back with far greater devastation. But what makes 'The Long, Twilight Struggle' more successful than its predecessor is the way it personalizes the conflict. It may be about the war between the Narn and the Centauri on the surface, but underneath it is really about G'Kar and Londo. G'Kar may be light years away from the fighting, but the intercutting between the scene of him praying and the battle at Gorash 7 places him at the heart of it. Meanwhile, Londo is forced to be there to witness the consequences of his actions as the Centauri fleet attacks Narn.

When Londo returns to Babylon 5, it is as the cold, hard Centauri ambassador. There is no trace of regret on his face as he parades around the Council Chamber laying down his demands with the assuredness of the conqueror. 'A wonderfully put together scene and I had a ball playing it,' says Peter. 'It's wonderful as an actor to get in a scene where twenty-five people have to sit and listen to you talk all day! [In real life] you get twenty-five of your friends together and you don't even get to the second paragraph before somebody says "Shut up!"'

But, again, the impact of the scene comes not from Londo's actions, but from the juxtaposition of Londo and G'Kar. It makes the conflict deeply personal with Londo representing the horror of the Centauri war machine as he lays down his harsh demands to G'Kar, its victim. 'Just a wonderfully constructed scene,' says Peter. 'I think Andreas had three or four lines in the whole scene and in a sense G'Kar really caps the scene. Londo, even at that moment of ultimate victory, feels how clearly he's been upstaged. He feels how the power of the scene, rather than residing totally in Londo where he feels it should be, is sliding around to G'Kar.'

'It gives me goosebumps watching it,' says Andreas Katsulus, who plays G'Kar. 'This is having your whole identity erased. My [G'Kar's] purpose for being there is suddenly erased, my status erased. It's almost like going home and finding your house robbed, everything is gone, you feel vulnerable. That speech he makes at the end is just dynamite when he talks about, "We will be free if it takes a thousand years." It moves me inside. [You can see] how the character's transformed: the old G'Kar would have resisted, but he's taking it in with a gentle determination.'

'I wanted everyone to feel for G'Kar,' says the director John Flinn. 'That's why I wanted to be right on top of him when he's doing all of that speech. I talked to Andreas, I said, "I'm going to be on top of you with this camera. I'm going to be less than a foot away while you're doing your speech. I want the world to see. I want everyone to feel." God, he just loved it. He took that and knocked me down.'

In the subplot, Delenn and Sheridan go down to Epsilon 3 at the request of Draal, and there is a little gift for viewers paying close attention. When Draal calls for one of his helpers who maintains the Great Machine, the name he uses is 'Zathras' which immediately brings to mind the eccentric alien seen in Season One's 'Babylon Squared'. Back then, all we knew was that Zathras was on Babylon 4 to take it through time to be the centre of operations in a war. Suddenly, Zathras is linked to Epsilon 3 and the Great Machine, although how and why would not be answered until season three's 'War Without End'.

Otherwise, the purpose of this subplot is a reminder to the audience of what lies on the planet below, and the immense power of the Great Machine. Draal gives Sheridan a little guided tour, puts the power of the machine at his disposal for 'the long, twilight struggle that is ahead', and then urges Sheridan and Delenn to leave as distress calls from the Narn/Centauri conflict start to filter through. In the original script, Draal was to make a return appearance in the final scene, where Sheridan is given joint command of the Rangers. It would then have made a clear link between those two plot threads and Sheridan's final speech about a line being drawn against the darkness. It emphasizes that the Shadows may have achieved one victory with their manipulation of the Centauri, but now Sheridan has the Great Machine and the Rangers on his side. 'There is so much dark in that episode,' says Joe Straczynski. 'I needed some shard of light to come in and say, "OK, there are possibilities for the future here."'

21:
'Comes the Inquisitor'

Click. Click. Click. The Inquisitor's cane taps the floor as he walks off the Vorlon ship. He steps out of the darkness to reveal a man dressed in nineteenth-century clothes. His name is Sebastian and he has come for Delenn.

Delenn steps into Grey 19 and the door clangs shut behind her. Two manacles slide across the floor and halt at her feet. Sebastian orders her to put them on, and she does so, ready for the test Kosh has sent her to endure.

'Who are you?' Sebastian demands. She replies that she is 'Delenn', but the Inquisitor hits his cane on the floor, sending a surge of energy through the manacles. Delenn answers again, that she is the ambassador for Minbar, that she is the daughter of— But Sebastian will not accept any of her answers and more pain surges through her wrists. 'How can you be expected to fight for someone else when you haven't the fairest idea who you are?'

Delenn stands isolated in a beam of light as Sebastian circles around her, mocking her belief that she has a destiny. 'How can you be sure,' he asks, 'if the world says otherwise? ... Perhaps the world is right and Delenn is wrong! Have you ever considered that?' She admits that she has.

G'Kar asks Sheridan for help. The other Narn on the station are beginning to doubt his abilities and only a message from his homeworld, from the family of one of the dissenters, can reverse that. Sheridan agrees to take the details and makes it his first mission for the Rangers.

Lennier finds Delenn in Grey 19, lying on the floor, exhausted from the pain and the questioning. She refuses to let him help her and so Lennier goes to Sheridan.

Sheridan enters Grey 19 with his PPG drawn. 'Leave her alone,' he says. Sebastian slams his cane down, sending a line of fire raging towards Sheridan, where it slams him up against the wall. Then Sebastian binds him against a metal grille and bombards him with questions. 'How many people are you prepared to sacrifice for victory? Are you willing to die friendless, alone, deserted by everyone?' Sebastian waves his cane in front of Sheridan and energy flashes across his face. Another question. Another energy burst. Questions followed by pain over and over until—

'Enough!' Delenn cries out from behind. 'If you want to take someone, then take me.' She approaches Sebastian, her eyes ablaze. She will not let him do this any more, even if it means sacrificing herself. 'If I fall, another will take my place,' she says. And with the demonstration that they are willing to die for each other alone in the dark, Sebastian releases Sheridan's bonds. They have both passed the test.

G'Kar is among a group of Narns, watching the message that Sheridan managed to get smuggled off the Narn homeworld. His chief dissenter smiles with gladness, relief and gratitude to see his wife and child. 'We will not question you again, G'Kar,' he says.

Sheridan escorts Sebastian to his ship, having discovered his history in Earth records. Sebastian lived on Earth in 1888 until he mysteriously vanished the morning after a string of murders in London's East End. Sebastian acknowledges that he was responsible for those 'unspeakable things' because he believed he was on a mission to end the decay, chaos and immorality that surrounded him. But the Vorlons found him, showed him his mistakes and how history came to regard him. 'Remembered not as a messenger,' he says, 'remembered only as Jack.'

The pain and torture that Delenn is forced to endure in 'Comes the Inquisitor' strips away the outer layers of the person she seems to be to get at the person she really is. The method Sebastian uses is one that the writer, Joe Straczynski, took from real life. 'It actually uses what's called the Synanon Game. There was a therapeutic model which kind of got out of control developed by [the US drug rehabilitation group] Synanon, where you ask a person "Who are you?" and they have to give a different answer each time and by the time you answer the question, you start to get down to the meat of it. It can be a very disorientating and disturbing game to play.'

Thus it proved for Delenn. This is the person who hitherto had been portrayed as gentle, religious and caring. Suddenly, she is thrust into a world of violence where Sebastian carries out his assignment with a shocking, cold viciousness. Over the course of the second season she had faced prejudice from Minbari and humans and been thrown out of Grey Council. Now she faces torture. 'She had to be sufficiently kicked and provoked to stand on her own two feet again,' says Joe. 'To assume responsibility and to put her own life on the line and, in a way, re-find her confidence. And that is, in measure, what the Inquisitor does. You may be the right person in the right place, but you have to be willing to do what is required of you. By the end of that rigour she was. It also reminded her what her cause was. The cause is not her fulfilling prophecy: the cause was life.'

It put Delenn at the centre of the story, giving a wonderful opportunity for actress Mira Furlan to play every emotion from vulnerability, to fear, pain, anger and defiance. 'I liked carrying the episode, the drama of the episode, on my shoulders,' she says. 'It was a good episode for me, as you can imagine – a lot of heavy drama was going on. It was a very well-written episode, I think, the gradual transformation and destruction of Delenn. But she's not destroyed. She wins that battle because of her strength.'

The interrogation scenes were powerfully presented with stark lighting and a great deal of movement from both the actors and the camera, which earned *Babylon 5* an Emmy nomination for cinematography. Mike Vejar directed the episode and decided it had to be done this way. So much screen time was devoted to the interrogation scenes that the usual method of cutting between a master shot and close-ups wouldn't have sustained the material. 'It was so powerfully written that I don't think it would have been represented well if I had just shot it in the standard way,' he says. 'It was mostly a psychological attempt to break Delenn and I felt the circling and the lack of a sense of up and down, back and forth, light and shadow, could be utilized to enhance the inquest and to set her ill at ease. So I tried to get a sense of vertigo in there with the camera moving around and turning at the same time he was turning, to try and get the audience to have the same sense of being thrown off balance that Delenn was going through.'

The torture effects were added later by computer and Mira Furlan remembers having discussions about what kind of pain Delenn was experiencing and where it came from. 'You had to imagine the pain,' she says. 'I imagined it as electric shocks for some reason. I imagined something that goes through your whole body and through your head which is like lightning.'

When Sheridan joins her, however, the line of fire that streaks across the floor towards him was actually created on the set. It was real fire, not a computer-generated image. 'I loved the thing when he just flashes me against the wall and I go flying up against the wall and down,' says Bruce Boxleitner. 'That was a great stunt. The stunt man did the basic thing, then I just came in and slammed myself against the wall for the tight shot. I had back pads and hit it as hard as I could without hitting my head and flew backwards into the wall. Then there was being tied up in some S- and M-type of thing,' he laughs. 'We knew there was supposed to be effects and we just reacted to it. When he passed that wand in front of me, I pictured electrical charges happening to me.'

Although, if truth be told, Bruce Boxleitner wasn't actually tied to that metal grille on the set. 'I could pull my hands away,' he reveals. 'I was actually holding my hands like that, trying to keep them up there to look like they were bound. I could have broken the bonds at any time. Listen, living here with earthquakes, if there had been an earthquake and everybody ran and left me standing there – not likely!'

Elsewhere, there was more drama for G'Kar. A moment of coincidence brings him and Vir together in a transport tube. Vir, ashamed at what the Centauri have done to the Narn, makes an attempt at an apology. In response G'Kar cuts into the palm of his hand and, as the blood drips out of it, he says one word over and over again: 'Dead, dead, dead ...'

'That was an incredible scene,' says Stephen Furst, who plays Vir. 'Andreas Katsulus is such an amazingly intense actor. It's such a pleasure to work with people like that. There are those actors who are good and charismatic and there are those actors who are just incredibly talented, and Andreas is one of those incredibly talented people. He can convey so much under all that foam rubber and prosthetics that he's an amazing person to watch. I'm a huge fan of his.'

'This isn't your enemy, this is Vir,' says Andreas Katsulus, putting G'Kar's motives into words. 'I've always considered him the enemy and he's making an offer of a certain kind. How can I explain to him how I feel? One is to completely smash him in the face and say, "That's what I think of your offer." But to show him how I feel to make it dramatic. To cut. Dead. I feel this way about every single Narn. The power of all this is so huge.'

The episode ends by revealing Sebastian's true identity to be Jack the Ripper, the notorious prostitute murderer of late-nineteenth-century England. Joe Straczynski decided to take the figure from history and place him in the *Babylon 5* universe because Jack's belief that he had a moral duty to cleanse society has some correlation to Delenn's belief that she is fulfilling prophecy. 'This is someone who – if you read his letters and if you read what he did – believed he was sending a message. He was a fanatic, and who better to test the fanatic than another fanatic? Someone who has shown that his beliefs were wrong and that he was doing it for the wrong reasons, and therefore was convinced that no one else could ever be doing it for the right reasons ... In a way he is also the subject of the inquisition, because she [Delenn] makes him confront these things in himself when she stands up to him and says, "What about you, Mr Sebastian?" She gets him mad because she's pointing out to him the things he doesn't want to face.'

The revelation that Jack the Ripper is the Inquisitor is the final twist in a catalogue of cruelty. Delenn seems to be being punished for no crime. If the inquisition is meant to teach her a lesson, then to do so by resorting to violence that could lead to her death is a lesson in the extreme. Sebastian is not simply, as it might appear, an inquisitor going beyond his remit: he is a murderer brought into the service of the Vorlons. And that reflects back on them. 'It makes you ask the question: if these are good guys, why send a torturer out in the first place and why this guy?' says Joe. 'Would God send Adolf Hitler to do something like this?'

22:
'The Fall of Night'

'There has been enough death. It's time for
something better,' says Mr Lantz, just arrived from
the Ministry of Peace to sort out the problem of the
escalating Centauri war. G'Kar is thrilled,
anticipating Earth coming to the aid of his people.
But Lantz is there to sign a non-aggression treaty
with the Centauri to keep Earth forces well out of it.

A jump point opens on the far side of Epsilon 3
and a battered heavy Narn war cruiser limps into
Babylon 5 space. It was out on patrol when the
Centauri hit its homeworld and now it is requesting
sanctuary. Sheridan agrees to protect the ship and
the captain takes the jump engines off line to divert
power to the medical systems. While the ship stays
on the dark side of the planet, it cannot be seen by
anyone. But the techs on C and C know exactly
what is going on and one of them is a member of
Night Watch.

A jump point opens and a Centauri battle cruiser
emerges, placing itself in front of the jumpgate,
blocking the Narns' escape route. Starfuries stream
out from the launch bay and form a protective
cordon around the Narn ship. Lantz is furious. 'This
jeopardizes everything I've worked for!' he protests.
But Sheridan orders him escorted off the
Observation Dome. The treaty hasn't been
formalized yet and Sheridan promised the Narns
sanctuary.

Sunlight streams across the Narn cruiser as it
lumbers out from behind Epsilon 3 and heads
towards the jumpgate. The Centauri react, sending a

spray of energy bolts towards the Starfuries and Babylon 5 itself. The security grid powers up and shoots everything out at the Centauri cruiser. A group of Starfuries peel away and rain down their weapons along its body. Clusters of explosions flare up on the Centauri ship, disabling it, as the Narn ship and an escort of Starfuries make it through the jumpgate. The damaged Centauri ship crackles from the inside and is destroyed in a ball of light and debris.

Sheridan, wearing his dress uniform, sits on the core shuttle on his way to the Zen Garden, where all the alien ambassadors are gathered. The shuttle stops at Station Two and all the other passengers depart while Sheridan is lost in thought over the apology he has been ordered to make to the Centauri. A tiny whine catches Sheridan's attention and he turns to see a bomb attached to the seat where a young Centauri had been sitting. His eyes widen. He barks at the computer to open the shuttle doors and dives out into mid-air.

The ambassadors in the Zen Garden look up as the shuttle explodes in a mass of fire. Silhouetted against the flames is the tiny speck of Sheridan's body floating down towards them. Ivanova screams into her link for a rescue crew with jet packs, but Sheridan is heading towards the ground spinning at sixty miles an hour and in thirty seconds he'll be dead. Delenn appeals to Kosh. 'You know what is at stake. If you are going to do anything, you must do it now.'

The head lifts from Kosh's encounter suit and Delenn looks up as a glowing Minbari figure with wings flies up towards Sheridan. 'Droshalla!' breathes the Drazi ambassador, seeing a Drazi deity flying above him. 'G'Lan,' says G'Kar, looking at a *glowing, winged Narn. Sheridan sees an angel with a human face. 'Kosh ...?' he asks as the angel reaches out its hand and brings him safely to the ground.*

There is the hint of Neville Chamberlain in the character of Mr Lantz, the man who arrives from the Ministry of Peace to sign a non-aggression treaty which, he claims, will bring 'peace in our time'. Chamberlain, British prime minister between 1937 and 1940, famously followed a policy of appeasement towards Nazi Germany and claimed to have brought 'peace for our time'. It all disintegrated for him, however, when Germany invaded Czechoslovakia and then Poland. 'There's always somebody ready to sell off somebody else as long as we don't have to worry about it,' says Joe Straczynski. 'It's definitely meant to capture that spirit and that time.'

The episode starts off as relatively low-key for a cliffhanging finale. There is even a little vignette between Lennier and Vir (actually carried over from 'Comes the Inquisitor') in which they express their feelings about their own ambassador while, paradoxically, their comments could just as easily apply to the other ambassador. 'It's like war stories,' says Stephen Furst, who plays Vir, 'talking to another actor about "I went to this audition and it was horrible and I was treated so badly". It's what everybody does and these guys are just two guys, ambassadors' assistants, and once in a while you just like to complain and you like to have company to complain to. It was a wonderful scene.'

The scene was filmed at the end of a long day and it was one of those times when all the producers were standing around, praying they were going to get it in the can before all the crew downed tools and went home. 'I'd been there probably since seven in the morning waiting to do that one scene and they're all looking at their watches trying to get it in time and it was a kind of a high-pressure moment,' remembers Bill Mumy, who plays Lennier. 'Anyway, Joe was there and – I'll never forget this – I said, "Come on, come and sit at the bar, be in the scene at the bar." He was like "no" and I was "oh come on" and he was like "no". I try to be a fun person, try to keep things light and I didn't really hear him so well and I was thinking, "Oh, he just wanted me to twist his arm." Finally he got really pissed off, it was like, "*No! I don't want to do it!*" He explained it to me, he said that he believes this show. When he sees it he believes it and he has to keep that belief system in place to write it and if he sees himself in it he'll stop believing it. He was very uptight about that because I was really insistent.'

Things begin to escalate when Sheridan sends out a fleet of Starfuries to protect the Narn cruiser, against the wishes of Earth as represented by Lantz. It provides the opportunity to round up the sub-plot surrounding Lieutenant Keffer that had been brooding throughout the season. His quest to find out more about the 'something' he saw in hyperspace in 'A Distant Star' reaches its peak here. On one level it kicks off another plot thread for the third season, when his footage of the Shadow ship is picked up by ISN, and on another it kills off a character who, despite being included in the opening credit sequence, never amounted to much. 'He was an OK character,' says Joe Straczynski. 'I could have kept him around if I chose to do so, but I just figured, "Let's keep up the ante here and let's fry him." In that piece, if you look at it frame by frame, we melted his face off!'

All this is minor to the grand revelation of the episode – and possibly the season: Kosh emerging from his encounter suit. 'I wanted the audience to say, "OK, this is a new episode, we've seen it before" and then beat the crap out of them!' says Joe. 'I tend to look at the audience as a living beast behind me and my job is to distract the beast so I can slip a story past and then rap them upside the head.'

Joe specifically wanted the scene to happen in the low-gravity environment that exists towards the core of the station. Babylon 5 creates gravity by rotation and so it is quite different from what one would experience on Earth if, for example, one happened to jump out of an exploding aeroplane without a parachute. 'When I was hearing about this, it was, "Wow, then I'm just going to drop like a rock, right?"' says the Sheridan actor, Bruce Boxleitner. 'They said, "No, don't you understand that you will float because it's only sixty per cent gravity as you get closer to the centre. But when you pass through the centre you start to speed up as you get closer to the ground at the opposite site. It would be like stepping out of a car going sixty miles an hour on the freeway – it would hurt!"'

It is a key moment that was part of the original story arc as conceived in 1986–7. Again, it is a revelation that does far more than answer the mystery of what hides within Kosh's encounter suit. He looks like an angel to human eyes, but other races see their own religious icon. That poses further questions about the Vorlons' influence on the development of these races and still doesn't tell you what Kosh really looks like. Furthermore, Kosh's decision to expose himself to save Sheridan expresses how important he believes Sheridan's life and his future role to be.

'One of the recurring images of this show is a hand reaching out for someone else,' says Joe Straczynski. 'We use that image in "Confessions and Lamentations" when Garibaldi picks up the sick Markab; later on in "Late Delivery from Avalon"; we use it also again in Londo's dream, in "Whatever Happened to Mr Garibaldi?" – again the hand reaching out to catch someone from a fall. And, of course, at the end of the third season we have him [Sheridan] in a fall and who will catch him this time? The metaphor behind that being if someone is falling [we should] try and catch them. It's a subtle thing, but I like doing it.'

The sequence was one of the most difficult special-effects sequences ever attempted by *Babylon 5* and required an extra day to be set aside to film it. 'That was really hard,' admits the director Janet Greek. 'We had extensive storyboards on that, and then of course we had to film everything on the ground. We put flying rigs on the actors and they had to get up in the rigs and do a bunch of stuff in the rigs and then the CGI stuff was painted in all around them. The really wide stuff – a lot of that was pure CGI. Some of it was me shooting an actor full-frame and then on the computer they shrunk it down for effect. The work Foundation Imaging did on that show was really amazing. That was a difficult show to do because it was so much of them and we were just providing them with a piece.'

'We were on cables, he and I,' remembers Bruce Boxleitner. 'They would take him down, put a new head on him and send him up again ... They were the last days of the second season, so it was time for the crew to relax and unwind a little more and sit around and reflect on the end of the season.'

Bruce Boxleitner came in with a tough job in taking over the lead of a show that had already been running for a year. He felt the weight of everyone's expectations on him at the beginning, and so to have made it through to the end was a nice feeling. 'Television is such an unsure thing. Maybe suddenly, halfway through, [they would have said], "We don't like Bruce Boxleitner" and the show's cancelled and we're all gone,' he says. 'I was, "Wow, a season's gone by, the first one is over." I felt very happy with it, the growth of the character and everything. I made it to the end and I never thought I'd see the end.'

BABYLON 5
FROM BOXTREE

Please send me copies of:

❑	07522 0252 9	A-Z OF BABYLON 5	7.99
❑	07522 0841 1	CREATING BABYLON 5	13.99
❑	07522 0644 3	NOVEL #1: VOICES	4.99
❑	07522 0649 4	NOVEL #2: ACCUSATIONS	4.99
❑	07522 0654 0	NOVEL #3: BLOOD OATH	4.99
❑	07522 0153 0	NOVEL #4: CLARKE'S LAW	4.99
❑	07522 0158 1	NOVEL #5: THE TOUCH OF YOUR SHADOW, THE WHISPER OF YOUR NAME	4.99
❑	07522 0163 8	NOVEL #6: BETRAYALS	4.99
❑	07522 2339 9	NOVEL #7: THE SHADOW WITHIN	4.99
❑	07522 2344 5	NOVEL #8: PERSONAL AGENDAS	4.99

TO: **Macmillan Distribution Ltd.**, Direct Customer Services, Brunel Road, Houndmills, Basingstoke, Hants RG21 6XZ, UK
TEL: 01256 302 699
FAX: 01256 64733

HOW TO PAY

Please charge my Access/Visa/Amex/Diners Club for £ _____

Account Number _____

Expiry Date _____

I enclose a cheque for £ _____ payable to **Macmillan Distribution Ltd.**

Name _____

Address _____

_____

Postcode _____

Signature _____ Telephone _____

FREE POSTAGE AND PACKING!
in UK and Eire only.
Please allow 28 days for delivery.
Prices and availability subject to change without notice.